D0595691

HAPPINESS

HAPPINESS

published by

SHAAR PRESS

Formulas, Stories, and Insights

by

RABBI ZELIG PLISKIN

Published by SHAAR PRESS
Distributed by MESORAH PUBLICATIONS, LTD.
4401 Second Avenue / Brooklyn, N.Y 11232 / (718) 921-9000

ISBN 10: 1-57819-454-7 / ISBN 13: 978-1-57819-454-4 Paperback

Printed in Canada

∽

I dedicate this book to

Rabbi Noah Weinberg

with profound gratitude

∽

ACKNOWLEDGMENTS

I wish to express my profound gratitude to the Creator for all that He has given me.

I thank Shmuel Blitz for suggesting the topic and format of this book. Working with him is a great pleasure. His speed in making things happen is amazing.

I am extremely grateful to Rabbi Noah Weinberg, founder and head of Aish Hatorah. His emphasis on happiness has had a great influence on me and a multitude of others.

My father, of blessed memory, was a wise and brilliant Torah scholar. I value all that he taught me more and more as the years go by.

My mother's love and devotion has had a major influence on me throughout my life. Her compassion has been a great teacher.

May the Almighty grant long life and good health to my wonderful in-laws, Rabbi and Mrs. Simchah Weissman. May they have much *nachas* from their children, grandchildren, and great-grandchildren.

I am grateful to all those who have given me feedback, suggestions, and encouragement on this project. I am especially grateful to: Rabbi Kalman Packouz, Michael Dorf, Mrs. Leah Richeimer, Mrs. Sarah Shapiro, and Uriela Obst.

TABLE OF CONTENTS

A Note to the Reader:

Stories throughout this book are written in the first person. Those in italics did not occur to the author himself.

INTRODUCTION

I was captured by an enemy who had one goal: to make my life miserable. I wasn't physically tortured, only emotionally. I was deprived of all enjoyment. I was given enough food to stay alive, but nothing more. I was subtly threatened as to what would happen to me in the future, and this filled me with worry and anxiety. I was made to feel guilty, lowly, and worthless. Insults and put-downs were constantly thrown at me. "If you have any feelings of hope about the future," I was told, "give them up. You will suffer for the rest of your life."

Wouldn't it be awful to be a victim of such an enemy? Unfortunately, many people are. And the enemy that is creating such unhappiness is themselves. They think and act in patterns that cause themselves intense, yet unnecessary suffering. The way they talk to themselves and the inner pictures they visualize cause them much emotional misery.

Is it possible to go from self-torture to a life of joy? My experience has proven that the answer is yes. You have the ability to create happiness for yourself regardless of what your emotional reality has been until now. Most people don't suffer as much as has been described here. But they have very limited emotional lives. They don't experience a fraction of the joy that is available to all those who learn to use their minds wisely.

You create your emotional reality in your brain. Create a life of joy. How? This book will show you. You are created in the Creator's image and deserve a joyous life. Don't rob yourself of this joy. Claim your birthright.

King Solomon in his wisdom gave us his formula for happiness. "A good-hearted person feasts perpetually" (*Proverbs* 15:15). The "good heart" is the heart of a person who consistently appreciates what he has. Such a person always has a reason to celebrate. This person can be you.

Everyone will agree that appreciating what you have is a valuable attribute. But it's easy to forget to put this into practice. We need daily reminders. Since my source book *Gateway to Happiness* was published in 1983, I have seen which formulas people have found most beneficial. I have also seen common patterns in people's thinking that prevent them from experiencing as much happiness as they could. The present book is based on my counseling experience over the past 25 years.

There are three basic principles that those who have mastered happiness apply regularly. Here they are in concise form. The rest of the book is just commentary.

Principle One: Appreciate and enjoy.
Principle Two: Find the positive.
Principle Three: Talk and act joyously.

These three principles are the foundation of happiness. Without following these principles, no matter what one has or does, one won't be happy. Reading about these three principles is just the beginning. Putting them into action, both mental and physical, is what will create a joyous life.

When you master these principles you will:

Make a total commitment to increase your level of happiness in life.

Appreciate all that there is to be grateful for in your life and your world.

Learn how to enjoy what you have not enjoyed doing before.

Find the positive in yourself, in other people, in experiences, and in your life situation.

Change what can be changed, but see the potential for growth and development in each encounter and experience.

Talk and act joyously for this will create inner joy.

Free your mind from counterproductive inner chatter and fill it with inspiring and motivating messages.

Visualize yourself joyously reaching your goals.

The doorway to a life of happiness is open before you. You have the guidebook in your hands. You will find formulas, stories, insights, and uplifting messages. Let them lead you on an uplifting journey. As you read and reread this book, these ideas and patterns will become an integral part of your thinking. After applying these principles regularly, people will be asking you, "How come you are so happy all the time?"

I.

WISH PEOPLE JOY

I was walking on a busy street and came upon a beggar. Everything about him projected the message, "I am poor. Have a heart and help me out." I gave him a coin and wished him well.

With a happy look on his face, he blessed me, "May you smile and laugh the entire year."

I felt that I gained more from him than he gained from me. This incident happened to me right after I had bought fish for the upcoming holiday and was headed for my publisher's office to sign the contract for this book. This was a great opening for a book on happiness, I thought to myself. I felt so good about this blessing that I reflected, "Wouldn't it be wonderful if these good wishes were on everyone's lips?"

When you wish other people, "May you have much joy," you yourself are getting in touch with your own joy. Saying this from the bottom of your heart accesses these feelings in yourself. As you bless people with happiness and joy, you might even recall your favorite joyous memories. Every time you remember those memories, they have the capacity to give you a lift.

"May you smile and laugh the entire year." Imagine yourself smiling and laughing the entire year. Wouldn't it be something if this were your everyday reality?

Yes, that beggar gave me more than I gave him. And if you pass on the heartfelt blessing of this anonymous beggar, the power of his blessing will be awesome. May you personally smile and laugh the entire year as you bring greater happiness to others.

What if you feel that as yet you don't have enough joy to spread around to anyone else? That is why we need many more formulas for happiness. When you finish reading this book, reread this section. Hopefully, your attitude will be, "My increased happiness has done so much for me, I wish to help others increase their happiness."

2

MASTER THE SKILL OF HAPPINESS

Everyone wants to be happy, but not everyone is committed to do what it takes. A true commitment to achieve happiness requires mastering the attitudes and actions that create it. This involves careful study and repeated practice.

When a commitment is needed, wishful thinking is insufficient. If you want to win a lottery, the first step is to buy a ticket. Imagine someone claiming that it is important for him to win the national lottery.

"How many tickets did you buy?" you ask him. "I didn't buy any," he replies. It is obvious that he is not serious about wanting to win.

There was an amazing story that recently occurred in Israel. It was reported in the newspaper and I verified it with an employee of the lottery company. A man had a dream that four specific numbers would be among the winning six numbers. In this lotto, the grand prize would be divided among all the ticket holders who accurately guessed six numbers that were chosen at random.

The man with the dream considered the dream a fantasy and did not purchase any tickets.

The following night he dreamt the same dream as the night before. He decided to take action. In this lottery when you bought a regular ticket, you had to guess all six numbers. But there were more expensive tickets that only required five numbers to be correct. He figured out all the numbers that he would need to choose for every possibility of a fifth number. He spent close to a thousand dollars to buy enough tickets.

That week the sum of the grand prize was 20 million shekels (approximately $5 million). Four tickets had the winning numbers; two of them belonged to him. This was the first time in Israel's history that any single individual had two winning tickets in a single lottery. His total commitment won him 10 million shekels.

Happiness is more precious than wealth. Commit your total self to master it. What will it take to make a strong commitment? Be aware of all the benefits of living a joyous life. Beyond all emotional, health, and material benefits, when you experience happiness and joy, you will be able to attain profound spiritual awareness and love for the Creator. And as the revered Chazon Ish wrote, "When a person merits becoming aware of the reality of the Almighty's existence, he will experience limitless joy. All of the pleasures of this world are as nothing compared to the intense pleasure of a person cleaving to his Creator" (*Emunah U'bitochon* 1:9; See *Gateway to Happiness,* pp.91-114). Additionally, it is necessary to be cognizant of all the drawbacks and suffering which result from unhappiness.

Happiness is up to you. You can create it or destroy it. Your intense commitment to master happiness will enable you to experience more happiness yourself and many others will benefit from the way you interact from a place of joy.

3.
HAPPINESS: YOUR BIRTHRIGHT

"I'm not happy. And my biggest problem is that I feel that I don't deserve to be happy. I don't consider myself to be evil. But I'm nobody special."

"I have many character flaws. I lose my temper too frequently, and I tend to be lazy. You can't expect someone like myself to be happy."

"I was told as a young child that I was a failure and wouldn't amount to anything. My deep feeling of unworthiness has prevented me from being happy throughout my life."

You were born. That is all you need to deserve to live a happy life. Happiness is a birthright. You don't have to be considered special by any other person to have a right to be happy. Every human has intrinsic worth and infinite value.

When you know that you have a right to be happy, a potential barrier to happiness is removed. Some people mistakenly feel that happiness is only for those who somehow deserve it. But where is the international committee that would make such decisions or has created criteria for who is deserving to be happy? In reality, all you need to do is realize that happiness is your birthright. The decision is totally up to you.

Not only is happiness a birthright, it is actually an obligation. As Rabbi Noah Weinberg, founder and dean of Aish Hatorah, constantly says, "Happiness is an obligation. You have an obligation to yourself to be happy, for when you are happy you will be healthier and will accomplish more. You have an obligation to other people to be happy, for when you are happy you will treat others better and will refrain from many forms of causing them distress. You have an obligation to the Almighty to be happy, for He is your loving Father and wants you to be happy."

When I first heard of the concept that happiness is an obligation, it did not add to my happiness, to say the least. I tend to view obligations as heavy responsibilities. Does this mean that when I am unhappy, I should feel guilty?

But then I realized that of course happiness is an obligation. It makes total sense that it is an obligation to myself, to others, and to my Creator. Feeling guilty about not being happy is not conducive to happiness and will not get me closer to my goal of being happy. But when I realized that I have a strong moral and ethical obligation to be happy, it increased my motivation to develop my appreciation for what I have. When I incur a financial debt, I work diligently to repay it. As a matter of fact, I feel good that I am a responsible person and am meeting my obligations. Now I view my obligation to be happy in the same way. I give myself credit for the effort I put into this project. Viewing happiness as an obligation has motivated me to help others meet their happiness obligation.

START YOUR DAY THE RIGHT WAY

What are your first thoughts when you wake up in the morning? Regardless of the past, from here on choose thoughts of gratitude. The more joy you experience in your life, the more gratitude you will have and the easier this will be for you.

"I am alive! I am alive!" you can shout each morning (to yourself in your mind, if others are still asleep).

Imagine several scenarios for which this thought would be the spontaneous reaction. Someone is involved in a potentially fatal car crash and he comes through unscathed. Someone inadvertently walks into a robber's crossfire with the police. Someone is kidnapped, threatened with being killed, and is eventually released unharmed. Someone is saved from drowning or survives major surgery.

You don't need such dramatic life events to feel happy you are alive. You can experience this exhilarating emotion many times each day. Especially when you first wake up in the morning, express your profound gratitude for the gift of life. Getting off to a good start sets the tone for the rest of the day. This is the power of saying the *Modeh Ani*[1] prayer the first moment you are awake: "I express my gratitude to You, the King Who is alive and always exists, for returning my soul to me, with compassion. Great is your trustworthiness."

If you do not yet spontaneously feel the joy of being alive, act as if you are joyous. See how this increases your good feelings. It can be helpful to do this with a light sense of humor. Individuals who are too earnest and serious when they try this complain that it does not work for them. The benefits of this joy are so great that it is worthwhile practicing until you find a way to make this work for you.

"There is always a context to the events that happen to us," my teacher, the late Rabbi Chaim Shmulevitz used to say. He would give the following analogy: If your glass falls and breaks, you might be upset. But if the moment this happens, a friend of yours comes and tells you the great news that you just hit the jackpot, you would be in a joyous state. In the context of winning the lottery, the loss of a glass and the hassle of picking up the pieces are trivial.

He would tell his students: When you gain a profound appreciation for being alive, you will be free from complaints. From the context of the intense joy of being alive, all that is difficult in your life will become easier. You will still need to seek solutions, but your emotional state will be more conducive to finding them.

If you are alive when you read this, give yourself permission to exclaim, "I am alive! I am alive!" Repeat this frequently throughout the day.

---

1. Traditional Jewish prayer said immediately upon awakening.

TAKE A DEEP BREATH

As you read this paragraph, you will be breathing. Be aware of your next breath. Every time you breathe, you can either breathe subconsciously or you can choose to breathe mindfully. And then you can choose to be grateful for each breath, which is what the Midrash suggests that we do. Since you breathe regularly throughout the day, the practice of being grateful for each breath will fill your day with gratitude.

There are courses on art appreciation and music appreciation. Breathing appreciation will enhance your life even further. Spend five minutes counting your breaths. This will increase your awareness of how often you breathe and will slow down your breathing.

When you breathe slowly and deeply, your nervous system relaxes and becomes calmer. Slow, deep breathing alleviates anger, tension, fears, and stress. These states are not conducive to clear thinking or happiness. As you breathe slowly and deeply your mind clears and you will be able to gain a broader perspective that is helpful in dealing with those underlying issues that have caused the distressful feelings in the first place. When you add gratitude, the process becomes much more effective.

I am often asked, "What is the one spiritual exercise that would help me connect with the Creator?"

"Breathing," I suggest.

"Breathing?" is often the incredulous reply.

"Yes, breathing! When you make breathing a spiritual experience, you gain a greater awareness of the Almighty's love and kindness. You appreciate that He gave you a need for oxygen so you would be constantly reminded that He is giving you what you need to stay alive."

We are all addicted to oxygen. Try to hold your breath for 30 seconds and the only thing you will be thinking of is, "I need my oxygen fix right away." This is a healthy addiction, and no one suggests that we give it up. Since you are breathing anyway, upgrade its quality. Be grateful for each breath. Begin right now with your next 10 breaths.

6.

APPRECIATE AND ENJOY

We each have much to appreciate and enjoy every day of our lives. What stops us? It's easy to take that which we already have for granted. We are excited with new things. We focus on the pleasure and feel good. After we get used to what we have, we tend not to focus on it any longer. We tend to focus on what we don't have. The Sages have taught, "He who has one hundred wants two hundred. And he who has two hundred wants four hundred." Focusing on what you are missing makes you overlook what you have.

Train your brain to become more mindfully aware of all that you can appreciate and enjoy. Be mindful of your ability to see. Be mindful of your ability to hear. Be mindful of your ability to talk. Be mindful of your ability to walk. Be mindful about your ability to move your hands, and to lift, pull, turn, press, and hold things with them. This alone will transform your life. The person who is mindful about these things will have a brain that is so full of appreciation and enjoyment that it will be free from many of the thoughts and pictures that create bad feelings.

Practice being mindful about each of your senses and basic abilities. Choose one a day. One day focus on appreciation for being able to see. Notice colors and appreciate their shades and gradations. Another day be mindful about your ability to hear. Be grateful for being able to hear people talk, either in person, on a telephone, or on tape. Be grateful for hearing music, for hearing birds chirping, for hearing anything that you enjoy to hear. Another day be grateful for your hands and all that they can do. When you turn on the faucet to have running water, appreciate your being able to make that motion. Be grateful for being able to get dressed. Be grateful for being able to write or type. Another day be grateful for being able to walk. Throughout the day appreciate your ability to stand up and move from one place to another. As you walk, enjoy the sense of movement.

Appreciate every possession that you own or can use. Be grateful for silverware and cups. Be grateful for watches and clocks. Be grateful for chairs, tables, and beds. Be grateful for your clothing and for the food you eat.

Imagine how appreciative you would feel if you were missing all that you have and then you obtained them one by one. This is a great exercise to practice when your mind is free and otherwise would focus on worries or on unhappiness producing thoughts.

Add a spiritual dimension of appreciating everything you have as a gift from your loving Father and powerful King, Creator and Sustainer of the universe. Appreciate His love for you and reciprocate by feeling love for the Giver of all that you have. Being immersed in these feelings will enable you to live a life of gratitude, happiness, and joy.

7

THE UNIVERSE IS YOURS

Would you like to gain immense wealth with only a limited amount of effort? You too can transform your wealth consciousness with just five words: View the universe as yours.

The Talmud (*Sanhedrin* 37a) teaches that each and every person in the world is obligated to say, "The world was created for me." This means that we are responsible for the world. Each individual has tremendous value. And this means that we should appreciate everything as being ours.

- When you see the sun, realize that it is your sun that gives you light and heat.
- Trees and flowers, mountains and lakes have been created for your benefit. They are yours to enjoy.
- The stars and galaxies add an expansive dimension to your world even if you never step foot on any other planet besides our own.
- Birds and fish, horses and cows, tigers and jaguars, giraffes and elephants, all are yours. Whether you see them daily or only once in a while, they are part of your immense fortune.

• The land and the sea, with everything on them and beneath them, are yours to benefit from and preserve for later generations.

You might be short of cash from time to time. But regardless of how much cash you have available, as long as you have the awareness that the universe is yours, you are wealthy. This wealth was given to you as a gift the moment you were born and it is yours for your entire lifetime. To claim this wealth, you just need to: "View the universe as yours."

"View the universe as yours," I was told.

"Who am I going to fool? I'm deeply in debt. My dreams are not to become rich, I just want to get by," I replied. I always felt deprived and missing out on what life had to offer. I needed more money, not this abstract concept.

But the person who suggested that I view the world as having been created especially for me was persistent. "This worked for me," he said. "Don't discount this idea without experimenting. Test it out for an entire week."

I realized that I didn't have anything to lose, so why not? After two days of viewing the sun and everything else that I saw as mine to enjoy and benefit from, I began feeling better than I had felt in a very long time. When the week was over, I felt like a totally new person. I had great energy and wonderful inner feelings. My mind was clearer than it had been in a long time and I thought of a plan to solve my financial difficulties. Yes, I really was wealthy. I had always been, but I just did not realize it before. I now try to spread this concept to anyone who will listen to me. Those who do are fortunate, very fortunate.

8.
WISE CHOICES

The family went to the zoo on a holiday with a taxi. There was a huge crowd and the taxi left the passengers two blocks from the entrance to the zoo. One person complained, "We paid for the ride. It wasn't right of him to make us walk like this." Another one said, "Look up at the beautiful scenery. See those interesting trees. And it's fascinating and exciting to walk here with all these other fascinating families."

A group of friends arrived at the bus stop just as the bus was pulling out. One said, "Isn't it awful that we have to wait now for the next bus!" Another said, "Now we have time to discuss the plans that we never have a chance to speak about."

The rain prevented them from following their original plans. One said, "It seems to always rain on our parade. Now the day is ruined." The other immediately asked, "What can we do now that we will enjoy?"

Two individuals were told that the airplane was overbooked and they would have to wait for the next flight. One sulked and felt miserable the entire time. The other spent the time reviewing some important ideas that he wanted to master and felt great about this unexpected opportunity to do that which he never seemed to find the time to do.

Realize that you constantly choose what your brain will focus on. Some people habitually focus on what is not to their liking, what is disappointing, and what is distressful about their situation or what they are doing. They have done this so often that they can mistakenly think this is their basic nature. It is not. It is just a habit that has become automatic. This is the opposite of what you need to do to master happiness.

Even during the most perfect day there will be something to complain about. Even during the most enjoyable experiences one's mind can create distressful feelings. There is a choice to think to oneself, "Isn't it awful that my average day isn't as good as this?" Or one can think, "This won't last." Or, "Yes it's pretty good, but it's not perfect."

Happy people make happiness-producing choices of focus. And they realize that they almost always have a choice. Even when things are not totally to their liking, they find ways to improve upon situations. When they cannot make any practical improvements, they choose to focus on life-enhancing thoughts. If the weather is uncomfortably hot, they keep their focus on more enjoyable topics. If plans do not work out, they immediately make new plans. If one door of opportunity is closed, they look for other doors that they can open.

Some people automatically blame and complain so much that they view that as total reality. "How can I not complain when things are not the way I want them to be?" they will ask. And this is in contrast to happy people who ask the opposite, "Since feeling good is such a high human priority why would anyone needlessly focus on what makes them feel bad when they can make positive choices?"

As an experiment, keep asking yourself, "What can I focus on now that is enjoyable?" Keep this up for an entire week. Even here an anti-happiness thought can jump to the forefront of one's focus, "Isn't an entire week a long time?" Or, "Isn't this hard work?" About the first question, if you will be alive for the next week you are experiencing life anyway, why not enjoy it? About the second question, when you really enjoy doing something, you focus on your enjoyment. Whether it is easy or difficult just is not an issue.

After consistently choosing thoughts conducive to happiness for a long enough time, it will become your second nature to do so. Exactly how long you will need to make a concerted effort until this becomes automatic, only you will be able to answer. And when you are able to answer this, you will see that all your efforts were worthwhile.

9

THE AMAZING POWER OF "NEXT!"

"How do I change the focus of my brain?" is a common question that people ask. "I tend to think of the negative. I worry a lot. My brain focuses way too much on thoughts that aren't conducive to happiness. How can I stop thinking about what I do not want to think about?"

A powerful tool that will help your brain move to the type of thoughts that you wish for is to tell it: "NEXT!" Then your brain will joyfully move on to another picture, idea, song, series of words, thoughts, imaginary scenes, visualizations, and anything else that brains like to do. Your brain can choose from an enormous amount of material that it already has stored in its immense library.

After you say, "Next," your brain might even choose a fantastic wonderful scene that it can create on the spot. Brains do this all the time when you are asleep. So whether or not you feel that your brain can really do this, know that it definitely can. All brains can and do during the process we call dreaming. When you are kind to your brain, it will be willing to do this for you when you are awake.

Try talking to it gently. Most brains prefer to be spoken to in this way. You might want to say, "Next, dear brain." Or, you might find that your brain responds better when it is given an authoritative order. Since you are its boss, you have a right to try this out. But I still would advise the softer and gentler approach if your brain responds well to it. If you feel you must be tough on your brain, yell the word: "NEXT!!!!" But if your brain goes passive-aggressive on you after you do this, it is your own responsibility for I warned you that the authoritative approach might sometimes backfire.

You might ask your brain for its personal recommendation. "Brain, how would you prefer to be spoken to when I say, 'Next'? Are you the tough type that wants to prove you can take it when you are spoken to sharply? Or would you prefer a soft, 'Next'?"

The more frequently you train your brain to respond to the word "next," the easier it will become for your brain to comply. When your brain listens to you and goes quickly to another thought, picture, or song, reward it with something positive so it will be motivated to listen to you in the future. The better you treat your brain, the more it will try to please you.

10.

ACT JOYOUSLY

Act joyously. These two words are powerful. They work. Test it out congruently and see for yourself how effective this formula is.

If it is so easy, how come everyone is not radiating joy? I did not claim it was easy. It is simple to say, but the very fact that not everyone consistently applies it shows that it does not come naturally to many people. It takes effort. And it also takes belief in the process. You can counteract the effects of acting joyously by holding back or by repeating to yourself, "This will not really work."

"Act with enthusiastic joy and you will actually experience it," was expressed by Rabbi Moshe Chaim Luzzatto in his classic work *Path of The Just* written in 1740. Since then many professionals in the field of human emotions have repeated this formula. It worked then and it still works now. The more flexible someone is with their emotions, the easier it is for them to apply this. Experiments with biofeedback technology and the testing of hormones in the blood after acting joyously have proven its effectiveness.

When something very special happens in your life, you spontaneously react with joy. Remember this feeling. Giving this state a name makes it easier to access it. Remember how you talked and acted when you were in this state in the past. And in the future when you want to experience more joy, talk and act the same way. Those who have experienced joy more frequently find this easier to do, but with a conscious effort everyone can learn to do this.

Personalities differ. Some people easily change their emotional states. As soon as they decide to act joyously, they immediately access this state. Their entire being is an expression of joy. On the opposite end of the spectrum are people who are much less emotionally fluid. For this to work for them takes more practice. But even they will gain by acting joyously. Their determination and persistence will eventually enable them to experience more joy.

When I first heard about the concept of acting joyously to experience joy, I was skeptical. The fact that so few people actually apply this gave me the impression that such joy was not real. I would try this out from time to time, but my lack of belief that this would work actually prevented it from working.

What changed my mind? I met someone I knew as a teenager and he radiated joy. "I remember you as being emotionally heavy," I told him. "How did you become so joyous? Is your life going so great or did you work on your emotions?"

"My life situation is not better than most people I know," he replied. "But I realized that when I acted joyously, I felt much better. A turning point for me was when I attended the wedding of a friend. As soon as the newly married couple entered the

hall in the middle of the wedding meal, all the guests immediately jumped up from their seats with great smiles on their faces and began singing and dancing. Nothing new had happened. The guests had attended the wedding ceremony. But the appearance of the stars of the wedding was a signal, 'Rejoice. Sing and dance. Your joy will increase their joy.' Of course, it is easier to do this at a wedding, with a large crowd and a band. But the same principle applies. As soon as you decide to act joyously, you have the ability to create inner joy. The more I practiced this, the easier it became. Now it is not an effort. But I do need to remember to act joyously. If I forget, invariably someone will remind me, by asking, 'Is anything wrong? You're not your joyous self.'"

Having my friend as a role model showed me that it could be done. Now my goal is to be a role model for others.

II

APPRECIATE PEOPLE

Right this moment, there are a multitude of people all around the planet involved in serving you. Many of them you will never meet in person, but you will benefit greatly from their activities.

There are farmers who are planting and harvesting for you. There are people in the clothing industry who are weaving the cloth and designing clothing you will eventually wear. There are trucks, boats, and planes that are shipping the food you will eat, the clothes you will wear, and many other items that you will buy or use. There are people who are involved in making certain that you have water, electricity, phone service, and books. The postal authorities are busy at work delivering the letters you sent and bringing you mail that others have sent you. There are inventors who are working day and night on items that will one day be yours. There are engineers, mechanics, and a wide variety of laborers all around the globe who toil for your benefit. There are medical researchers working to find cures for illness that might one day save your life.

Whenever you see a large crowd of people, it is a reminder to be grateful to all of those who are involved in one way or another in enhancing the quality of your life.

When you meet people, even in passing, whose job or profession benefits you in any way, tell them that you appreciate what they do. This will give them a good feeling and help you develop a greater amount of appreciation.

For example:

"Thank you so much for delivering my mail. You keep me in touch with my family and it means a lot to me."

"I appreciate your teaching the children of our city. You are preparing the next generation to live a good life."

"So you work for the sanitation department. Thanks a million for making our city more pleasant to live in."

"I would like to express my gratitude for your keeping our neighborhood safe. Even when I get a driving ticket, I appreciate how the police force protects me and my family."

THE ART OF REFRAMING

One of the most important skills to master is the ability to find realistic, positive reframes. The quality of your life is the quality of your reframes. Because of its importance for living a happy life, we will discuss it again here even though it is dealt with at length in several of my books *Marriage; Anger: The Inner Teacher;* and *Begin Again Now.*

Let us define the word *reframing.* Events, situations, and occurrences in themselves do not cause you happiness or unhappiness. Events just happen. It is always your personal, subjective evaluation of those events that create your emotional reaction. If you evaluate, or reframe, something as neutral, you will not be effected emotionally. If you evaluate, or reframe, something as negative, you will experience either sadness, annoyance, frustration, anger, distress, or suffering. If you evaluate, or reframe, something as positive, you will experience happiness, joy, serenity, relief, or pleasure. It is your own way of thinking about something that creates your emotional reaction. Even if others evaluate something as positive, you can evaluate it as negative. And even if others evaluate something as negative, you can evaluate it as positive. It's all up to you.

You are constantly reframing, either consciously or unconsciously. We all have an initial reaction to things. If your original reframe was positive, great. If not, you can then reframe, or reevaluate, the way you perceived what happened.

A master at positive reframing will live a happy life. He or she seeks out positive reframes before, during, and after events, situations, and experiences. Even if it is difficult to find a positive reframe for an unpleasant event, it can still be experienced many ways. For example, "I'll be glad when it's over." "I'm grateful that my life is usually better than this." "This is adding depth to my character." "I will devote my life to help prevent others from this suffering."

As I was in the middle of writing this, a friend of mine called me up to tell me that he has a reframe to share with me. He was attending a lecture and someone in the audience called out a few minor, technical corrections. At first he felt bad for the speaker who he assumed might have been annoyed with the interruptions. But then he reframed it, "The speaker could feel good that the person was listening so carefully to everything he said." I asked my friend, "Does this mean that you are becoming more of an expert at reframing now?" "It's always easier to reframe for others," he replied.

Depending on your entire life history, you will either tend to be a positive reframer or a negative one. Those people who had an early environment with positive reframing will usually find it easier to find positive reframes throughout their life. But even if you grew up in an environment of negative reframes, it is never too late for you to begin to master positive reframes.

Here are some questions to ask about events and experiences that will help you master the skill of reframing. When you become an expert, you won't have to make an effort to think of positive reframes. They will be your automatic reactions.

- *What is good about this?*
- *How can I grow from this experience?*
- *How can I find a long-term benefit from what happened?*
- *What character trait can this help me develop?*
- *Why is what happened not so bad?*
- *What are some creative possibilities how later events might turn this into something positive?*
- *How will I look at this in a year, ten years, fifty years?*
- *What is humorous about this?*
- *How can I use this for spiritual enlightenment?*
- *How could I reframe this for someone else?*
- *What would an expert reframer say about this?*

13

YOU HAVE WHAT YOU NEED

"I have exactly what I need," the Torah master told a former student of his.

The student, who had not seen his teacher for a number of years, visited him to seek advice on a complex matter. The student was financially successful and was grateful to his teacher for what he had taught him in the past and for the advice he had just given him.

"My dear teacher, my business is going well and I would like to repay you. Please accept a check from me as a token of my gratitude."

"My beloved student," the great spiritual teacher replied, "I see that you sincerely want to give me a large amount of money. But I truly have all that I need."

"But look how few amenities you have in your house. And everything you do have is old," the student insisted. "Please take this check. I already have enough money to retire. It would give me great pleasure to help you out."

"But I don't need to be helped out. What I have is exactly what

I need to have to fulfill my mission in life. I will be very pleased if you gave the money to a young couple about to get married who need to set up a home. But I lack nothing."

The spiritual awareness that you have what you need is a foundation for happiness. You might feel you need more and have a right to put in the effort to try to acquire what you wish. But before, during, and after your efforts realize that whatever you have is exactly what you need. When you truly need more to fulfill your life's mission, you will get it. But the Power Above is the only One Who really knows when and what that is. Your trusting Him will ensure you a happy life.

14

THE GRAPES YOU CANNOT REACH MIGHT REALLY BE SOUR

There was a fox who loved grapes. One day he saw a bunch of ripe grapes hanging from a vine. The fox jumped into the air to reach them, but could not jump high enough. The fox kept jumping, but after 10 tries and misses he realized that he would not be able to eat them for that day's lunch. As the fox walked away, he said to himself, "It's just as well that I could not reach them. They were sour and I did not really miss out on anything."

This famous fable is often used to describe the "sour grape syndrome." If a person cannot have something, he defensively assumes it was not worthwhile having in the first place.

For those who want to live a happy life, this parable has much to offer. If someone wanted grapes but could not have them, perhaps they were not as good as they looked.

I would like to suggest some updated rewrites of the story of the fox and the grapes:

• The fox said the grapes were sour, but really believed that they tasted good, so he felt bad. He wanted to hide this from himself and others so he just said they were sour. A tall bear came along later that day and was able to reach the grapes. He had to spit them out because of how sour they were.

• Another fox came along and when he saw he could not reach them, he piled one rock upon another until he could reach them. He fell down from those rocks just as he was about to reach the grapes. Not only didn't he eat the grapes, but he injured himself in the process, unlike the first fox who gave up and was able to find other food.

• A bear came along and reached the grapes. They were the best grapes he had ever eaten. He ate so many of them that he got sick.

• A few moments after the fox left the scene some fox hunters came along. They ate some grapes, but missed out on shooting the fox who unbeknown to him had a very narrow escape. If he were to have lingered to eat the grapes, he would have become a fur coat.

• The grapes were really good. But our friend the fox found another vine that he could reach and enjoyed himself more than he would have with the original grapes. The grapes he did find were tastier than any on the other vine.

• The fox couldn't reach the grapes. "I accept my Creator's will," he said. And this was the beginning of the fox's path to spiritual enlightenment. In the future, he was grateful to the Creator for the grapes he did eat and accepted with serenity anything that did not work out the way he preferred.

The moral of the stories: If your original plan does not work out, enjoy the plan that does. The original plan might not have been as enjoyable as you thought. It might have caused problems you did not anticipate. What you actually do could be better for you in the long run. And as you obtain acceptance of the Creator's will, you will live a more joyous life.

15

THE ULTIMATE HAPPINESS FORMULA

The ultimate happiness formula is trust in G-d. This trust gives you peace of mind. This trust transforms your life and adds a spiritual dimension to all that you do. Sincere trust in G-d makes you wealthy. If others just think you have this absolute trust, it's like others just thinking that you are wealthy. If you say the right words but do not yet feel them, it is like saying, "I am wealthy," before attaining actual wealth.

How do you know when you need to increase your trust in G-d? When you worry about the future, hear the inner message: "Trust in G-d." When you are intimidated by another person, hear the message: "Trust in G-d." When you are upset about the way something turned out, hear the message: "Trust in G-d." When you do not attain what you wished for, hear the message: "Trust in G-d."

If you were to have financial difficulties and a reliable wealthy influential person tells you, "Trust in me that I will help you out," you would feel calmer. If you were to have a legal problem and an experienced brilliant and trustworthy attorney would say, "Trust in me that I will help you out, and I guarantee you that things will work out well," you would feel calmer. If you desperately needed an airline ticket and the head of an airline told you, "Trust me that you will be all right," you would feel calmer. These are your metaphors for trust in G-d. Having this trust makes you calmer.

We cannot know exactly how events will turn out, but we can know that they will turn out in a way that will be in our best interests. And when you consistently have this awareness, you will consistently live a happy life.

Prayer is your most powerful tool for increasing your trust in G-d. Besides formal prayers, pray from your heart in your own words. As you connect with the Creator, you will experience the benefits with greater tranquility and peace of mind.

I used to think that I could do it all alone. It took a major crisis to teach me that I was powerless myself. Trust in G-d saved my life.

I was always a top student. I was intelligent, creative, popular, and successful. When I went into business, my business prospered. I was the kind of person that everything I touched turned into gold. I had an expensive home where we had many guests, receptions for fund-raising, and public lectures. My wealth and home were a major part of my identity.

Trying to expand my business, I took some risks that did not work out the way I wished. My business failed and I had to sell my house to pay off debts. I felt tremendous stress all the time. I could not sleep at night and I lost my appetite. Finally, I collapsed while walking along a busy street and I was hospitalized.

I appreciated my friends who visited me and gave me encouragement. One visitor said something that changed my life. "Trust in G-d," my friend told me. "You carried too much of a burden because you felt you were the one who did it all. Trust in G-d and let Him carry your burden."

This, of course, was not new to me. But in intensive care I had the biofeedback machinery to see immediately the calming effects of experiencing this trust. I felt calm for the first time in ages. I lost my business and my home, but I gained peace of mind and a greater sense of spirituality. Eventually my health improved and my business flourished. I now had the greatest partner possible. I had no guarantee that I would be wealthy, but I was assured a happy life.

16.

DEVELOP A WIDE THRESHOLD OF O.K.NESS

Happy people have a vast amount of things that they consider to be o.k. We all have our limits. But we can develop attitudes and reactions that enable us to accept, tolerate, and ignore many of the things that annoy, irritate, and frustrate unhappy people.

Some people need things to be "just so" for them to feel comfortable and happy. The more rules and specifics that are needed for this, the more likely that a person will experience much unhappiness.

Are there any people you dread interacting with? Those with a low threshold of o.k.ness are often in this category. They demand that everything has to be exactly as they wish it to be for them to be satisfied. These people are highly critical of others. They get annoyed at others for minor and trivial matters that are not to their liking. Do not be one of them for your own benefit and the welfare of those who interact with you.

Develop a sense of perspective. Keep asking yourself, "How important is this for me to fulfill my life's mission?" The clearer you are about which values are truly important to you, the easier it will be for you to accept and cope well with trivial and minor aspects of life that are not just the way you would have wanted them to be.

When I was a child, I demanded that my food should be prepared just right for me. It was the same with everything else in my life; my clothing, my room, the weather, how people speak to me, and the list went on and on. My mother could not tolerate the temper tantrums I often threw in order to get her to do whatever I demanded. My mother's giving in to me trained me to make a fuss about whatever I did not like. I manipulated people with my "out of control" behaviors. But deep down I knew that I could control others to meet my needs.

When it was time for me to get married, I wanted to marry someone who would go out of his way to make me happy. All potential candidates were tested to see if they would be devoted to making me happy. But everyone I met failed my test. They felt that my demands were unreasonable and unacceptable.

Finally, I met someone I wanted to marry. We were engaged and I appreciated how flexible he was. I would tell him what I wanted and he would do whatever I asked. Several weeks before the wedding he canceled our engagement. "You have such arbitrary rules for making yourself happy," he said. "You demand that I walk on eggshells. Maybe you can find someone who will keep bending to make you happy. But it won't be me. I'm glad I realized early enough that I can't take it anymore."

I was shocked and stunned. I felt furious at him for doing this to me. Then I realized that I did this to myself. I had made my happiness dependent on things being exactly to my specifications. I realized that I needed to be much more flexible.

To change my pattern, I tested my own limits of tolerance. I engaged in a strict schedule of depriving myself of things I used to think I could not do without. I cut down drastically on what I ate. For three whole months I roughed it, living as ascetically as I could. After three months I started living normally. My going to the extreme showed me that I could live happily with much less than I had ever thought. Now I am really ready for marriage and life.

17

MAKE MUSIC IN YOUR MIND

"When you attend a wedding, take the band with you," the Rabbi of Lublin, Rabbi Meir Shapiro, advised his students.

Rabbi Shapiro was a creative leader and educator and mastered joy in all circumstances. His deathbed scene has become one of the most famous in Jewish history. He constantly taught, "Everything we do in life, we should do with joy. Even dying." So as he was breathing his last breaths, he asked his students to dance and sing around his bed. What an amazing teacher! With one statement, he taught them how to live and how to die.

Wherever you are and wherever you go, you can create a mental symphony orchestra. If you prefer, you can create a lively band playing simple tunes. And as you become more of an expert at this, you can increase the amount of musical instruments you will see and hear in your brain. You can have as many drums as you wish, if you enjoy booming loud music. You can have pianos or violins, harps or guitars, horns or accordions, and any unique combination you choose.

Maimonides, the brilliant codifier of Torah law who was also an expert physician, advised people who felt sad, "Listen to music." In our day, we have tape recorders and compact discs and do not need to wait until we can hear live musicians. But it will not always be appropriate to play a tape recorder. When the orchestra or band is in your brain, however, you can play any song you want any time you feel like it.

Intensify the sound in your brain to energize you. Play slow, soft music to relax and calm your nerves. Even people who cannot carry a tune can create their own music. Since only you will hear it, the only person's tastes that need to be met are your own.

18.

WHAT DO YOU ENJOY?

Happiness is doing the things you enjoy doing, and enjoying the things that you do. A person who is a master at creating a happy life will develop the ability to find a sense of enjoyment and meaningfulness in the daily activities that are not necessarily their preferences. A student who enjoys studying is fortunate. A person who enjoys his job or profession is fortunate. A person who stays at home most of the day and enjoys the tasks and activities is fortunate. But we all have things that we enjoy doing the most. These are the things that consistently put us in positive states when we do them.

Write a list of things that you enjoy doing. Find opportunities to do them. Recall times when you were in a positive state and what put you into that state. Add to your list when you find yourself enjoying something new or when you remember things you used to enjoy but now rarely engage in. Below is a partial list to begin with.

- *Reading books: Underline passages that are especially meaningful to you and reread them.*
- *Listening to educational and inspiring tapes*
- *Listening to your favorite music*
- *Talking to friends*
- *Writing letters or rereading favorite letters that you received*
- *Acquiring new knowledge*
- *Singing or dancing*
- *Swimming, running, or walking*
- *Meeting new people*
- *Doing acts of kindness*
- *Watching sunrises and sunsets*
- *Telling humorous anecdotes*
- *Listening or reading lighthearted literature*
- *Talking to people who are upbeat, understanding, insightful, or interesting*
- *Visiting interesting places*
- *Taking hikes*
- *Sitting in a beautiful garden*
- *Building your vocabulary*
- *Learning a foreign language*
- *Asking questions or getting your questions answered*
- *Playing with young children*

- *Teaching reframing*
- *Recalling your favorite memories*
- *Analyzing dreams*
- *Discussing deep ideas or debating*
- *Reading or hearing stories*
- *Learning a new skill or developing your talents*
- *Meditating on peaceful words*
- *Taking mental vacations to all types of places around the world. Since this exists in your imagination, you can visit distant places in just a few moments.*
- *Keeping a diary*
- *Looking at your old pictures*
- *Writing articles, essays, or poems*
- *Collecting… (Many possibilities to choose from)*
- *Teaching people how to be happy*

Whenever you feel down, ask yourself, "What do I enjoy doing that could help me feel better right now?"

19.

MODEL AND MIRROR JOYOUS PEOPLE

How did you learn as a young child? You observed how the other people in your environment spoke and acted, and you modeled or mirrored it. You were not taught to do this; you did so naturally.

To see modeling in action, watch how a younger sibling of 2 or 3 notices what his or her older brothers and sisters are doing and models it. This came so automatically to us when we were little that most adults do not realize to what extent they did this when they were young children. Maimonides (Laws of *Daios*) writes that the very nature of human beings is to be influenced by the people in their environment. Therefore we should choose positive role models from whom to learn.

The Sages (*Ethics of the Fathers* 4:1) define a wise person as one who learns from everyone. A wise person definitely makes it a top priority to live a joyous life. Learning from joyous people is the way to do this.

When you mirror someone, you will access the same state as they are in. This is when you copy the facial expressions, posture, tone of voice, speed of talking, even the rate of breathing of another person. When you mirror an angry or sad person, you experience anger or sadness. When you mirror a joyous or serene person, you experience joy or serenity. Some people tend to do this spontaneously. They automatically take in the physiology of others and enter the same states as those in their environment. When this is used positively, they have great rapport and empathy with others.

When you are in the presence of joyous people, consciously mirror them. Breathe the way they do. Smile the way they do. Move your hands the way they do. Talk as joyously as they do. Quite rapidly you will be feeling similar feelings to theirs. When you keep this up, you will be modeling them even when they are not present.

Some people are concerned that they will not be themselves if they do this. You will always be your own unique individual self. You will be happy or joyous in your own way. Learning joy from others is a skill like other skills. When you learn how to write, you will still write those things that come into your mind. When you learn to speak a foreign language, you will speak with your own accent. The same is with joy.

Think of three joyous people to model and mirror. If you cannot think of any, it shows that your environment needs more joyous people. Be committed to be a role model of joy for them. The fastest way to teach someone else how to become more joyous: Enter a joyous state yourself and ask that person to mirror you. You will be amazed at how fast this works.

20

THE JOY OF CHARACTER DEVELOPMENT

"I'm afraid to hear any criticism about my character."

"When I see that I have spoken out of anger or arrogance, I feel devastated."

"I tend to deny that I have done anything wrong. It would be too painful to admit even to myself that I have a negative trait."

"I'll be the first to agree that I have some negative traits. I am frequently eaten up with guilt about this, but that doesn't help me improve."

All of these people have one thing in common. They all need to learn how to appreciate opportunities to develop their character.

We all start off as young children who need our characters to be molded. We all have our natural areas of strengths and areas that need fixing. Anyone who lets his character traits go on automatic pilot will have many character failings. To have faults is the normal human condition. That is why we were put on this earth:

to develop and grow.

Allow yourself to feel joy with every action you take to develop your character. When you notice that you have a fault, be glad that you recognized it. Whether you find it yourself or whether someone else points it out to you, you can feel a sense of appreciation that you are aware of it, for now you can correct it.

You would never want to lose your wallet or purse. But if you do lose it, you will be glad that you noticed it was missing for then you can begin the search to find it. You have a right to feel the same way when a character failing comes to your attention.

It takes moral strength and courage to be open to improve yourself. As you keep developing this attribute, you have another source of joy.

"Thank you for pointing out that I was speaking in anger. I am working on conquering anger, and want to be able to speak respectfully even when I do become irritated or annoyed."

"You're right. I was inconsiderate. Your giving me feedback is going to be helpful."

"I still don't like to make mistakes. But I feel good that I feel bad. It shows that my values are important to me."

"I agree with you. That was a stupid thing to say. It's people like you who care for my total welfare and have the courage to say the truth that enable me to become a better person."

21

WHY NOT DO IT WITH JOY?

"I don't like doing housework, but I end up spending a lot of time doing it."

"I keep stalling about doing my reports. They are a real hassle."

"The entire time I am at my job I keep thinking, 'I can't wait until the workday is over.'"

There are many tasks, jobs, and chores that we will end up doing whether we really enjoy doing them or not. Many hours of our lives are spent this way. The late Rabbi Chaim Friedlander, of Ponevezh Yeshivah, used to say, "If you are going to do it anyway, do it with joy."

One of life's challenges is to transcend boredom. This is a distressful state. It does not have the same intensity as high levels of anxiety and fear. It is not as strong as depression and anger. But boredom is painful. There are many ways to make potentially boring minutes and hours more exciting.

Boredom can be quite easy to get out of. Suppose that you are listening to a class or lecture that you find boring. Your mind has spaced out. But then there is a fire alarm and loud cries of, "Fire! Everyone out."

You will go immediately to a much more exciting state. Or suppose that in your bored reverie you think of a creative idea that you feel might earn you a fortune. That will change your state. Or suppose that your brain suddenly runs through your 10 most favorite memories. And it does so with great intensity. It can even add music and vivid colors. Then your state will change. Or, you might even find a way that knowing the information will make a major difference in your life. For example, a teacher might say, "The points I am about to say will be on your final exam. I want each of you to know it well for it will help you in your life in general, and on the next test in particular." Look around the room and you will see interest on the faces of the other students.

If you are presented with a task that you reframe as being boring, your brain has a number of choices of how to go from a state of boredom to more exciting states. Your brain might find ways to think about something else that is much more interesting as your hands are involved in the boring task.

You might find something exciting about doing the task that you did not think of when you first started doing the task. For example, you can run races with yourself. You can time yourself for 10 minutes at a time and see which of a series of six 10 minutes will do the job the fastest.

You can listen to music as your body carries out the tasks. Most people find this easier to do when listening to an outside source of music. Some people have learned how to play music inside their own brains and therefore are able to listen to any music they remember as many times as they want and as loud as they want.

Some people create interesting conversations with imaginary

people. At times these conversations can be very enlightening and insightful.

If possible, find ways to delegate tasks you find boring to others who would enjoy it more. This is the famous reframe of Tom Sawyer who had other boys pay him for the privilege of whitewashing a fence that he personally preferred not to do. By acting as if he enjoyed what he was doing, he created a positive reframe for them. They felt and actually were getting their money's worth when they paid him to do something for him that he did not want to do.

You might be able to think of ways to earn more money doing things you do enjoy and then pay others to do what you find emotionally difficult.

Before you complain about having to do something you find boring, use your brain to find a solution. The solution you do find might be yet another source of increased happiness.

I used to find my job boring until I heard about the toll-booth attendant who had a party each day in his toll booth. He would play loud music, and would sing and dance throughout the day. When asked, "What are you doing?" he would share his secret, "I'm having another party. This is a great job." Since then I have also noticed many modified versions. These are the toll-booth attendants who say something cheerful to every person who drives by. I now do something similar myself. I am a clerk and what I do is routine. But since I keep thinking of something kind or pleasant to say to each person I interact with, my job is much more enjoyable. My mind is more stimulated and I appreciate the positive ways that others respond to what I say to them.

22

SMILE AT MIRRORS

Develop a loving friendship with mirrors. Every time you look in a mirror smile to it with a genuine smile. Mirrors love this. They will reward you with a smile in return. But they will only smile to you the type of smile that you smile first. Mirrors have this pattern. I've spoken to some and asked them if they would smile to me even when I do not feel like smiling to them. But they all nonverbally communicated to me that that is not the way they have been programmed. They will only smile to me the way I smile to them. Maybe you will find a mirror that will take the initiative to smile to you first. Perhaps you can experiment. Frown to a mirror and see if it smiles to you. If that does not work, see if it will smile to you if you wave and smile to it.

People are a bit like mirrors. They tend to reflect the energy you send their way. If you express sincere love, compassion, and concern, they are likely to reciprocate. But unlike mirrors, people are more moody and independent. Some might even smile to you even if you do not smile to them. Some might even keep this up over many years. But don't count on it. Humans whose brains have mastered the skill to do this, live joyous lives, since so many people do actually reciprocate.

After you have seen a number of mirrors smiling to you, you might not need an actual mirror as much as you did when you began. Some brains have found that they can imagine smiling to a mirror and see what the mirror would have shown. The owners of these magical brains find it enjoyable to imagine this daily. Brains that practice this daily are fortunate. The muscles of the face that smile send them more oxygen and therefore the brain is rewarded with a wonderful feeling. Some brains have even become addicted to smiling. Maybe yours will.

23

COMPARED TO WHAT?

A person can potentially use comparisons to mess up his life. For example, a person can go to the most elegant restaurant which employs the greatest chef. He can order the most expensive food. Then for the rest of his life he can say about any other meal, "This isn't as good as the meal I once had in that five-star restaurant."

I recently related this example to a group of tourists. They laughed. And then one spoke up and said, "I just realized that I do this all the time. Just last night at the fancy hotel where we were staying, my first comment after the meal was, 'This wasn't as good as the food I ate at another restaurant five years ago.' I didn't realize how foolish this response is."

Our brains constantly make comparisons. Some things are better than others. Other things are worse. We make major decisions based on comparisons. One's choice of renting or buying a house is based on comparing what is available at a particular price and deciding on the best choice for our specific needs. What school one goes to is based on comparing what is available and choosing the school that will be best for us. Making wise comparisons is a sign of intelligence.

Our patterns of comparisons will either be a way we prevent ourselves from enjoying what we have, or a way by which we gain a greater sense of appreciation. A sage once said, "In spiritual matters, look up and raise your sights. But when it comes to material and physical matters, look down." That is, in spiritual matters keep looking for role models to motivate yourself to reach higher and higher levels. But when it comes to appreciating your possessions and your financial situation, look at those who have less than you and gain a greater sense of appreciation for what you have.

With this idea in mind, I told a chronic complainer, "Whenever you are about to complain about anything, first think of a few ways in which your situation could be worse. Experiment with this idea for two weeks and see what happens."

At the end of two weeks he told me, "If I was cold, I visualized how awful it would be if I were in the North Pole without a warm coat and this made me feel better about my present situation. If I felt hot, I visualized how uncomfortable I would be in a desert without any water. And this made me feel better about my present situation. If someone yelled at me, I pictured myself being punched and beaten. And this made me feel better about my present situation. If I lost a small amount of money, I thought about how awful I would feel if I lost everything I owned. As I kept doing this, I would feel tremendous relief that my actual situation was nowhere as bad as what I could conjure up in my imagination. This has added a sense of perspective to my life that I was missing before. My complaining has drastically decreased."

24

TRANSFORM YOUR PROBLEMS INTO GOALS

"I have a problem with low self-esteem."

"I have a problem that I don't get along well with other people."

"I have a problem that I'm not as educated as I would like to be."

"I have a problem that I don't have as much money as I need."

"I have a problem that I don't accomplish as much as I know I could."

When I hear these types of statements, I often say, "I can give you a tool that will help you eliminate your problem with amazing speed."

"Really? But that seems impossible," is a standard reply, either said explicitly or implied by the look on the face or the tone of voice of the listener.

"Transform your problems into goals," I suggest to those who I think will be open to this approach. And when someone does accept it, there is an immediate lessening of stress.

Then the above statements are changed to:

"I have a goal to experience self-esteem and create a positive self-image."

"I have a goal to get along better with other people."

"I have a goal to become better educated. If I can't go back to school, I can still read, listen to lectures in person or on tape, or find a tutor."

"I have a goal to earn more money."

"I have a goal to accomplish more."

Problems cause anxiety, stress, and tension. Problems are debilitating as they deplete one's energy. Goals, on the other hand, are energizing and motivating. A valuable goal creates enthusiasm. When you picture yourself attaining your goals, your emotional state is elevated and you can even experience some of that future joy in the present.

At times, your goal might be to grow from your problems. Your goal might be to cope gracefully and with dignity. Your goal might be to deepen your character and create a wiser sense of self.

Right now make it your goal to think with the outcomes in mind. The Sages (*Tamid* 32a) define a wise person as one who anticipates the outcome. The outcome of changing problems into goals is that you accomplish more and feel much more alive and energized. Many things that used to be "problems" will now find their solutions. So the words to keep handy are: Goals, Outcomes, Solutions. These words represent patterns of thought that will transform your life.

25

ENTHUSIASM AND PERSISTENCE SCORE GOALS

What would your life be like if you reached all of your goals? Think of how much you and others would benefit and gain. No, I cannot suggest a way to guarantee that you will quickly and unswervingly reach those goals. But I can suggest two qualities that will make it more likely for your goals to be transformed into reality.

Enthusiasm and persistence. Repeat these two words (well, actually three) over and over. Allow yourself to remember vividly moments when you felt enthusiastic. Remember the power of enthusiasm. If you cannot remember a time when you were enthusiastic, then enthusiastically make it your goal to experience this wonderful attribute. Observe people who have high levels of enthusiasm. Allow yourself to plug into that powerful source of energy. Enthusiasm is contagious. So consciously catch it.

A key reason why people do not reach reasonable goals is because they give up too soon. But when you increase your level of persistence, this will not be true for you. For example, you might make it your goal to be consistently joyous. Some people who do this find it more difficult than they imagined. So they divert their attention elsewhere. In short, they give up. Persist! Don't give up. Keep trying. Enthusiasm is the fuel that gives you the energy to persist.

If you knew for certain that you could reach your goals, what goals would you make for yourself? This well-known question is powerful. It has changed lives. And now let its power change your life.

The Talmud states that a person will be led on the path that he truly wants to travel on. What path is this for you? How far along this path will you go? This depends on your enthusiasm and persistence. Right this moment be resolved to become even more enthusiastic about reaching your most important goals. (Or become more enthusiastic about formulating your goals.) Be resolved right now to persist along the path. Don't just sit down in the middle of the road. Don't get sidetracked and wander to the right or left. Persist. Keep going. Regardless of your speed, when you persist you will eventually get there.

Let it be said about you: Here is a person who enthusiastically persists and therefore the goals that were set have turned into accomplishments.

26

ENJOY THE PURSUIT

"When I establish a successful business, then I can be happy. Until then, I feel tense and nervous."

"When I get married, I'll be happy. But until then, I don't see how I can be happy."

"When my book is published, then happiness will be mine. But until then, the entire process causes me a lot of stress."

"When I finally finish school, I'll be happy. But until I graduate, you can't expect me to be happy."

Setting and reaching goals enables you to accomplish. An extremely common error is to think that you have to wait to reach your goals to be happy. The solution is to enjoy the entire process.

Anyone who really wants to accomplish will set new goals as soon as present goals are reached. This means that only by enjoying the journey towards reaching goals will such people be happy.

"But what if I don't reach the goals that I set for myself? How can I be happy if I'm not certain that I will actually reach my goal?" some people ask.

When you set a goal for yourself, you have a better chance of succeeding than if you had not made a goal for yourself. But you never have a guarantee that you will reach a specific goal. Experiencing positive emotions while working on your goal will usually give you greater amounts of energy with which to work on your projects. And it will be much easier for other people to get along with you when you are calm than if you would be highly stressed and nervous. If you don't reach a goal, no problem. Just set another one.

My husband was impossible to speak to when he was in the middle of a major project. He was so nervous and tense. He would raise his voice to me and the children for minor annoyances. When he finally reached his goal, he was pleasant for a week or two. But then he would work on another project and again he was difficult to deal with. I insisted that he go for counseling.

He claimed it was not his fault. It was my fault. It was the children's fault. It was his boss's fault. But then he blew up at a policeman who gave him a ticket for speeding. The judge censured him for speaking to the policeman the way he did. When my husband claimed it was not his fault, the judge told him that he must go for counseling to learn how to deal with stress.

My husband and I went together to a family counselor who quickly got a picture of the problem.

"How much of the time do you spend on working on goals and how much of the time do you just enjoy the fact that you reached your goals?" the counselor asked.

When my husband tried to give an honest answer, he saw that the majority of the time he was working towards a goal. If he kept up his present attitude that he needed to feel stressed out whenever he was trying to reach a goal, he would feel much stress and tension and very little satisfaction.

The counselor said that there are two type of drivers. There are drivers whose only goal is to get to their destination. They do not like the trip at all. They only want to get to where they are going. They suffer during the trip and this spills over to when they finally reach their destination. And then there are drivers who enjoy the scenery wherever they are. The entire trip is part of their adventure. The same applies to attitudes towards all goals.

My husband is very logical and this made sense to him. He told both the counselor and myself that he was going to be committed to enjoy the entire process of setting and reaching goals. My husband's strength of character and dedication to a mission enables him to reach his goals. Now he started using these same qualities to enjoy himself while he was working towards a goal.

I remember the day my husband told me, "It's amazing how much I am enjoying myself daily. It was really crazy of me to make myself and the entire family so miserable just because I was working towards a goal."

27.

USER-FRIENDLY MOTIVATION

If you had the option of choosing to be on the team headed by one of these two coaches, which would you choose?

"You're doing an awful job so far. You are a failure. If you keep this up, you will ruin your life and be totally miserable. How can you be so stupid? I've never seen anyone worse!" ("STOP IT ALREADY!!!" Right?)

"You are improving. Keep it up! You've made a lot of progress already, and I know that you will continue to make even more progress. Learn from each mistake and you will succeed. See yourself reaching your goals and all the benefits that will be yours. Feel the great energy that this will give you right now."

And what if these were not outside coaches, but the way an individual talks to himself? Anyone who talks to himself in ways that are similar to the first pattern will cause himself much anxiety and distress. Yes, it might even motivate some people to improve. But many who talk to themselves this way will become discouraged and will feel like giving up. These patterns wreak havoc with one's self-image. The stress and tension caused by these so-called motivational messages will have negative effects on one's emotions and health.

When you motivate yourself, do so with the same language that you would want someone else to motivate you with. When you motivate yourself with visions of reaching your goals, with encouragement, and with statements of belief in yourself, you will energize and empower yourself. This will increase your level of happiness at the same time as it will enable you to accomplish more.

Be aware of how you speak to yourself in general, and what you say to yourself when you try to motivate yourself in particular. People who motivate themselves with heavy criticism likewise tend to do so with others also. Even if someone finds that this works better for himself than a softer approach, it is still not the pattern of choice when trying to motivate children and students. The harm to their self-image could be devastating. Choose positive words of encouragement. Believe in the potential of children, students, and anyone else you want to motivate. And speak to them in a way that will motivate them to believe in their own potential.

I am an educator and part of my job is to motivate my students both in their studies and in helping them build their character. I used to feel that if I was soft, they wouldn't take me seriously. I am hard on myself and although many of my students would think I am tough with them, I am really easier on them than I am on myself. Some students would drop out, and I would blame them for not being serious enough.

Then one day I read a book called The Delicate Balance which described how children should be spoken to with positive wording instead of negative wording. I tried this with my students and I was astonished with how my positive wording was so effective. When I motivate my students with positive, outcome wording, they tend to speak to themselves this way. They become joyously motivated and both their studies and character are improved along with their becoming generally happier throughout the day.

28

WHAT IS YOUR TIME ZONE?

"I keep focusing on the troubles I've had in the past, and that prevents me from enjoying life."

"I worry about what the future will be like, and this prevents me from enjoying my life."

You actually live your life one second at a time. Each day we have 86,400 seconds to spend as we choose. After you delete the amount of time you are asleep, you have quite a lot of seconds each day. Invest your seconds wisely. Use them for appreciation, gratitude, joy, accomplishing, growing, and developing your character. This will enable you to live a good life yourself and will enhance the life of others.

Even if your past seconds were not spent the way you would have wished, with the present level of your brain's understanding, you can make positive choices this very second. Do not allow the past to cause you a loss of your present and future seconds. You can never know what the future seconds of your life will be like.

But as your brain masters the ability to make the most of present seconds, you will be able to be calm about the future. When the future becomes the present, your brain will make the best use of those seconds as they are experienced one by one.

If you feel overwhelmed, realize that you only need to handle and cope with one second at a time. You never have to deal with two seconds at once.

In the present you can choose words and actions that will enhance your life. In the present you can focus on joyous thoughts. In the present you can reframe things in ways that enable you to enjoy more and suffer less. Each second that your brain chooses wise words, actions, and thoughts it gains greater expertise in doing this. And then additional seconds will be spent wisely and joyously.

When your brain allows itself to be totally in the present moment, it is a fascinating experience, especially when you are surrounded by many people. You will observe and notice things that you otherwise might have overlooked. Your relationships with another individual will be based on the way both of you are in the present and will be free from the static of the past. You will be able to focus on what you need to at this very moment. When you study, you will concentrate better.

To be totally in the present moment means that you can look at whatever you see without judgment or evaluation. You just see and then see even deeper. Suddenly what is foreground and what is background can keep changing. You see what you are looking at as an artist or photographer would. You might see in a way that you never saw things before. This brings out your creativity. And this can bring out a feeling of oneness with the scene and ultimately with the entire universe.

One exercise I often suggest to people to build up their ability to focus on the present moment is to keep repeating:"Now I am aware..."You look at various objects in the field of your vision, and begin each sentence with the words,"Now I am aware..." In order to do this, you need to keep your mind on the present. Try it out. It can come in handy at times.

29

CAN YOU FIND LOST TIME?

I once met someone who was highly agitated. He had lost some time and now felt bad about it.

"But," I said, "the more time you spend on worrying about that lost time, the more time you will lose in the present."

"But if I'm not upset about it, that means I don't value my time," he replied.

"No, it's the opposite," I argued. "The more time you spend worrying about the lost time, the more time you will be losing in the present. So not being upset about the lost time shows that you really do value your time."

"But because of what you just said it means that I should now be upset and feel guilty about the time I lost while being upset about the time I already lost."

"But this just adds to your losing more time," I said.

"Are you telling me that each time I lose more time worrying about the time I already lost, I should keep adding those guilty feelings to the feelings that I already feel?"

"No," I pleaded, "stop being upset about your lost time. The time you spend on this keeps adding to the amount of time you lose."

"I see that you are right and this makes me feel even worse," he replied.

"Do you feel good or bad when you keep up this pattern?" I asked him.

"I feel awful," he replied.

"And how would you like to feel?" I asked him.

"I would like to feel happy just as everyone else would," he intelligently said.

"Since the more time you are upset about lost time means the more time you experience distress and not happiness, it makes sense to stop this pattern and change it."

"But why should I change it?" he asked. "It's right to feel bad about lost time, since lost time is lost forever and can never be regained."

Seeing that this pattern wasn't working, I decided to leave this form of dialogue. In its place I said something that he found funny. He smiled and laughed.

"Do you enjoy laughing?" I asked him.

"Of course," he said, "everyone does."

"What else have you found funny?" As he began answering this question, his face glowed and he kept laughing.

After he did this for 10 minutes, I said to him, "Do you realize that you have laughed for the last 10 minutes? If you keep replaying this and you keep on laughing each time, you will be able to create so much humor and laughter in your brain that your endorphin level can rise whenever you wish it to."

"Oh, I can't just make myself laugh," he argued.

"But I just saw you do it."

"I know. But who says that I can keep this up?" he asked.

"Who says you can't?" I replied.

"Just because I can't prove that I can't doesn't mean that I will ever laugh like this again."

What I saw was that his brain, like everyone else's, really had a choice. It could choose to make obsessive negative loops, wasting more and more time. Or his brain could choose to make enjoyable, humorous loops. And this way his thinking ability would be enhanced and he would be able to think of ways to make the best use of his time right now in the present. It was easier for him to make distressful loops. But he had the ability, just as you do, to make the effort to choose enjoyable loops and chains in his brain. What his choice will be, I do not know. Do you yet know which pattern you will choose?

If you said yes, terrific. It means that you know that you have a choice. And once you realize you have a choice of creating your own loops, most likely you will make enjoyable choices. If you said, "I do not know yet which choice I will make," it still shows that you believe that you have a choice. Then you might have said that you really do not choose, your brain does it on its own. If you said that, I'm certain your brain might have been offended. "Why do you think that I am mean and want you to suffer?" your brain can ask. Be kind to your brain and let your brain be kind to you. Choose joyous and enjoyable patterns for your brain. Your brain will repay you in kind and supply you with an unending series of enjoyable thoughts. And this will be conducive for answering the famous time-management question: "What is the best use of my time right now?"

30

YOUR MAGNIFICENT BRAIN

You are the owner of a magnificent brain. Wherever you go, your brain is always with you. You have a lightweight multimillion-dollar-value machine that you take with you at all times. You use this machine to study, to enjoy life, to relate with other people, to make money, to face tests and challenges. Your brain is powerful. If you are reading this, it is your brain that is enabling you to do so. Your brain receives images of the symbols that you are looking at and turns them into words and sentences. Because similar letters and words are stored in your brain's immense library, you are able to make sense of these words and can benefit from them.

The sheer number of pictures, knowledge, and information stored in your brain is awesome. When you think of how relatively small your brain is and what it has stored away in its cells, it is mind boggling. Whenever you recognize someone it is because that person's picture is stored in your brain. If you recognize any scene, whether you saw it in person, or in a newspaper, book, or magazine, it is because there is a picture of that scene in your brain. This can include gigantic areas and a wide variety of places.

Some people tend to just complain when they cannot remember something and take remembering for granted. A person who sincerely wants to master happiness will do just the opposite. Appreciating the power of your brain will give you thousands of joyous experiences.

Isn't it remarkable that my brain keeps me breathing even when I do not think about it!

Isn't it remarkable that I can remember the faces of so many people! (Even people who claim not to be very good at remembering faces can recognize thousands of faces. Can you recognize a picture of George Washington, Abraham Lincoln, Albert Einstein, even though you never met them in person?)

Isn't it remarkable that my brain can visualize so many scenes!

Isn't it remarkable that I can read and write!

Isn't it remarkable that I can recognize so many songs!

Isn't it remarkable that I remember so much information!

Isn't it remarkable that I can create new sentences!

Isn't it remarkable that I can recognize so many tastes and smells!

Not only does your brain contain so many pictures and so much information, your brain also contains a wealth of inner resources. Every moment you experienced joy, enthusiasm, humor, vibrant motivation, courage, self-mastery, compassion, creativity, serenity, and serene empowerment is stored in your brain. And knowing that these states are stored in your brain makes it easier for you to access them more often. As your brain remembers specific instances of when you experienced them and your brain enables you to see what you saw, hear what you heard, and feel what you felt when you experienced them, you will be able to reaccess them once again. And this is yet another one of the magnificent things your brain does for you.

31

FREE UPGRADES FOR YOUR BRAIN

When you upgrade your brain in any single context, you get a free upgrade in each and every context of your life. When your brain enables you to feel confident and empowered when interacting with one person, your brain can enable you to feel this way in all contexts. If you can be creative in one area, your brain can be creative in many similar areas. If your brain can concentrate when you read one thing, you can concentrate in other areas as well. If you were able to cope well with a specific difficult person or difficult situation, it means that the inner resources that enabled you to do so are stored in your brain and your brain can access them with other people and situations. When you are able to create or access the states of happiness and joy at will, it means that your brain can do this over and over again in many other contexts.

When you keep upgrading your brain, you will be free from much of the distress and pain caused by a brain that was not upgraded. Failing to upgrade your brain is the root cause of much suffering and many limitations. The more you upgrade your brain, the more you will transcend and create a better life for yourself and others. An upgraded brain increases your emotional intelligence and enables you to utilize more of your cognitive abilities. You will experience more joy. You will make and reach more and greater goals. Your interpersonal relationships will be enhanced. You will have better expertise in reaching people. In general you will be more efficient with less effort. Your general state of energy will be increased. You will know how to motivate yourself and will have greater self-mastery in all ways. As you continue the process of upgrading, be prepared for many pleasant surprises.

This one upgrade, that all upgrades can be used in all contexts, is one of the most powerful upgrades possible. Each thing you learn will be a resource for much more learning than you can imagine. And now, allow yourself to experience your brain upgrading itself with this concept: "Every upgrade to my brain is now available to me in all contexts of my life." This perspective about growth and development will spontaneously create positive changes in behavior and emotions.

I remember the first time I shared this idea with one of my married sons. He told me that he automatically does this. He is very confident, he is always very upbeat, he does not become depressed even when faced with adversity, and he uses his brain wisely. When I was his age, I did not automatically do this, and that is one reason why I am so enthusiastic about the idea of upgrading our brains in all contexts. People who find that in some places and with some people they automatically use more of their resources, and the discrepancy between what they are able to do in various contexts is very great, have a strong need to transfer contexts. This will make major differences in a wide range of areas.

Think of ways that you feel limited and stuck. What inner resources would you need to become unlimited or unstuck? It might be confidence, courage, creativity, serene empowerment, persistence, humor, or other similar resources. Think of a time when you had the inner resources that would be helpful for you now and apply them to times and in ways you previously have not. Every time you read this, you can think of even more ways to use your inner resources. And each time you apply an inner resource, your brain will find it easier to access it once again. Not only will this help you now; it will continue to help you in the future.

Everyone has moments of greater clarity and inspiration. Your brain has probably experienced this a number of times. After each such moment your brain is upgraded. Even if a moment of clarity and inspiration doesn't last in its entirety, it serves as a beacon of light that shines on the road. This enables you to see further down the path and makes your journey a bit easier. As your brain contemplates what it has gained from past moments of clarity and inspiration, you will be able to upgrade new moments with the same light.

An upgraded brain learns from each person it encounters. You can now remember different people you have met in person or seen on film, and use them as role models for the positive patterns that will enhance your life. If you have seen someone doing something positive even once, no matter how long ago, that picture is in your brain's great treasury. And now it is yours to follow any time you choose. As you integrate positive patterns, qualities, attributes, emotions, reactions, and reframes, you are upgrading your brain. And all this will become part of your identity and everyday reality when you allow it to.

PALM ON YOUR FOREHEAD

The previous section discussed the benefits of upgrading your brain in all contexts. When you want to remember to upgrade your brain in all contexts, past, present, and future, place your right palm on your forehead. Then say to yourself, "My brain is presently upgrading itself with all strengths, inner resources, and positive patterns, in all contexts."

The action of putting your palm on your forehead is powerful in creating the feeling that all the neurons of your brain are communicating with one another, "I want to share any new strengths, inner resources, and positive patterns that I have acquired." Each neuron will thus be able to gain greatly from every other neuron. If you can be confident when you are in a room by yourself, you can also feel this way when you are with others. If you can be joyous in one context, you can do so in all contexts. If you can feel empowered when you are in a room by yourself, you can also feel empowered when you walk into a room of strangers. You can add your spiritual feelings to all contexts. You can add your learning ability from one context to another. You can upgrade in love, respect, compassion, creativity, motivation and every other area.

When you have just accomplished something that you feel great about, place your palm on your forehead. When you feel especially serene or joyous or confident or courageous or creative, place your palm on your forehead. When you experience self-control or self-mastery in any area, place your palm on your forehead. When you find yourself having a positive pattern that you were not aware that you had before, place your palm on your forehead. Feel that pattern being available to you in all situations and with all people.

When you wish to access an inner resource or positive pattern that you do not have immediately available in a present situation, but you have had it in another situation, place your palm on your forehead. When your palm is on your forehead, feel those inner resources and positive patterns coming together so they will be ready for you to use right now. And if you are feeling resourceful as you read this section, place your palm on your forehead to create an inner mental upgrade. The more often you practice this the more effective it will be.

You might find that from time to time you would want an extra special tool for upgrading your brain. Then you can place one hand on your forehead and place the other hand on the back of your head. This adds to the experience of upgrading your entire brain. Try it with an open mind and feel the benefits.

Right now you can even view the past with your present resources. Visualize how your present awarenesses and inner resources would have upgraded your abilities and patterns in the past. Rerun those scenes with your present strengths and abilities and feel grateful that you presently have those abilities and patterns. By doing this you will find that those inner resources are more readily available to you. When you think of the past from now on, you want to be able to use it all as a resource. And you will, when you visualize yourself reacting in the past with the way you would want to, now that you know all that you know. When your brain is open to doing this for you, you will gain immensely in all areas of your life. Right now see yourself gaining in a specific area that you need the most.

You might not always find it appropriate to place your palm on your forehead. Therefore you can create an imaginary mental button on your forehead. This will be a mental button that when touched will enable you to access all of your mental resources and strengths. This is a button that will give you access to all of the empowered states that you have ever experienced. The benefit of the button trigger is that you can move your hand towards your forehead and touch that "button" without anyone realizing what you are doing — unless they read this book. And then they may give you a warm smile of recognition, for they might do this also. And if anyone says anything negative to you about this, your brain can say to itself, "I see that this person's brain needs an upgrade." And if that person's brain realizes that this will be your reaction, it is more likely to hold it in check.

33

IDENTIFY YOURSELF AS A HAPPY PERSON

"I'm a joyous person."

"I'm someone who loves life."

"I see myself as an appreciator of all the gifts the Creator gave me."

"I used to view myself as a sad person who is sometimes up. Now I view myself as a happy person who is sometimes low."

Your identity creates you. And you choose your identity. Yes, your childhood, your parent's view of you, the way others have treated you, who you compare yourself with, all have had a part in creating your identity. But it is only because now in the present you have decided to keep the identity you have been influenced to have. And if you have not made a conscious decision how to view your identity, you are still making a decision, albeit a passive one.

You might already view yourself as a happy, joyous person. If so, great. If that is not yet your picture of yourself, it makes sense to start viewing yourself this way now. All you need is one moment of happiness or joy to consider yourself as one.

Take a look at the negative side. If someone robbed only one person, we consider him a robber. A murderer only needs to kill one human being to get this hideous label. Let us utilize this basic concept for gaining a positive identity that works for us. If you were creative even once, you are creative. If you experienced confidence or courage even once, you are a person with this trait. Of course, you need to learn to access your creativity, confidence, and courage more often. But once is already a start.

When you perceive yourself as a happy person, you remember other times when you felt happy. And the more memories you have of happiness, the easier it will be for you to view yourself as a happy person.

Do not wait until you are happy 51 percent of the time. All the more so, do not wait for happiness 90 percent of the time, or as some do, 100 percent of the time. "If I am not always happy, how can I view myself as a happy person?" The answer is that once you are happy or joyous, you now have that experience in your life history. So you can easily view yourself, "I am a person who has experienced happiness."

Even if it takes a leap of faith, start viewing yourself as a happy person, who enjoys life and appreciates the Creator's gifts. And you can start this very second. So hear an inner voice making the statement, "I am a happy person."

34

A SENSE OF ACCOMPLISHMENT

"I have all that I need, but my life seems empty."

"I waste a lot of time and I feel overwhelmingly frustrated."

"I am involved in a few projects, but I never seem to complete anything significant."

We all need a sense of accomplishment. People who enjoy their involvement in studying, working, hobbies, or tasks that give them feelings of accomplishment are the happiest. A person who has all that he needs, but is not accomplishing, is likely to feel bored, empty, frustrated, or irritable. Being involved in meaningful accomplishments gives your life a sense of meaning and purpose.

There are as many ways to accomplish as there are people. There are the type of things that most people will view as an accomplishment, and there are quieter yet heroic accomplishments. Accomplishments include: gaining knowledge and wisdom; being part of a worthwhile organization as an employee, volunteer, or donor; learning new skills or mastering old ones; overcoming handicaps and limitations; coping well with illness or injury. What is an accomplishment depends on you the individual and your unique circumstances and situation.

There are many accomplishments that were major at one time and now are taken for granted. Learning to read and write is one. Learning how to stand up and walk is another and so is learning how to talk clearly enough that your early caretakers could understand what you wanted.

Goals lead to accomplishments and that is the importance of mastering the ability to set and reach goals. If you do not yet have meaningful goals, make it your goal to find one or a few.

Keep in mind that character development and spiritual goals are ultimately the most fulfilling. Trivial goals are better than not having a goal. But do not limit yourself. The greater your goals, the greater your potential for accomplishment and the more fulfilling your life.

It has been said, "When you have a why to live, you can overcome any how." That is, when you experience your life as meaningful, you are more able to transcend difficulties and hardships. Keep your eyes on making and reaching goals. If one goal does not work out, create another. And realize that you might already be involved in accomplishing something worthwhile, but you take it for granted. Make it your goal to appreciate past accomplishments and to find the potential for accomplishment wherever you are.

35

THE QUALITY OF WAITING TIME

"I hate to wait!" a busy executive confided in me. It wasn't really a secret since his annoyance was readily obvious to anyone who ever saw him wait.

"So you have eliminated it from your life?" I jokingly asked him.

"I wish I could. I dread waiting for anything or anybody. I start climbing the walls if I am kept waiting. I want to be on the move. I want to accomplish. Waiting is such a waste of my precious time."

"You're a successful entrepreneur. What are some of the key elements that enabled you to succeed?" I asked him.

"I am aware of my priorities," he replied. "I know what will give me the greatest returns for my investment of time and money. And I avoid spending time on things that will only benefit me minimally."

"Why do you want to earn large amounts of money?" I asked him.

"I feel that I can give a lot to others when I have enough money. But I have to be honest and admit that my main reason is because I want to be happy, and I feel that the more money I have the happier I will be."

"It seems to me that you can still add to your awareness of your priorities. You told me that you want to be happy. Isn't it ludicrous to make yourself miserable over time spent waiting when what you really want is to add to your happiness? It is not more money you need most. Rather, you need to view time in a way that wherever you are that is where you will find your happiness. Since you will always have to wait, it makes sense that you should make it part of your priorities to enjoy waiting time. Of course, you do not want to waste time. But when you utilize your waiting time wisely, it will not be wasted. At the very least, waiting time will add to your level of patience. And when you master patience, you will be free from much frustration and anger. You can carry a book with you that you will read when you need to wait. You can write letters. You can meditate. You can even utilize your waiting time to think of the best things to do with your waiting time. You might be surprised at all the creative possibilities."

I saw from the look on his face that he was ready to face this challenge. Two weeks later, he called me up and told me, "Thank you. I no longer have 'waiting time.' The time I used to view as waiting time is now time I spend enjoying life. Exactly what I will do depends on the circumstances. But I would not have believed how this change of perspective has saved me from so much aggravation."

Think of some of the things you personally can do to enjoy and gain from the time you spend waiting.

36

ANCHORING YOUR EMOTIONS

"Every time I hear this wedding song it brings back wonderful memories."

"Seeing this picture reminds me of the breath-taking scene I saw on top of the Rocky Mountains and I feel exhilarated."

"Touching my watch makes me smile as it reminds me how I look when I smile at mirrors."

"Moving my hand straight ahead automatically puts me into a focused state."

"When I raise my right hand and say, 'Yes,' I feel empowered."

The above are all examples of anchoring — the neurolinguistic word for associations that elicit responses. Unfortunately, many people associate this concept with Pavlov's famous dog that was trained to associate food with a bell and then reacted to the sound of the bell as if it were food. The reason why this is unfortunate is because anchoring is a positive tool that can be used to enhance everyone's life.

We all automatically have numerous anchors, some are pleasant and others are distressful. Pleasant anchors are anything that you see, hear, or touch that elicit pleasant feelings. Unpleasant or distressful anchors are things you see, hear, or touch that cause bad feelings.

Words are essentially anchors. The symbols you see elicit different feelings. Words — such as joy, happiness, serenity, relaxed, empowered — elicit memories of times you felt this way. And this affects your present state. For some people this is minor, while for others this can be intense. And the same applies to those words that elicit negative feelings.

People you like are positive anchors. Just mentioning the name of someone that you love, deeply respect, or find funny, will elicit a reaction of good feelings. For example, when a grandparent hears the name of his or her grandchild, you will often see a smile on the grandparent's face. When someone smiles or waves to you, you feel good because your brain associates these sights with positive feelings.

Phobias are when you associate danger with something harmless. It could be that you had a frightening experience that created that anchor. Or you just imagined something dangerous happening, even if the probability is very low. A person who is afraid to speak in public views speaking to a crowd as a distressful anchor. For those who love to speak in public this is a positive anchor. You can begin to enjoy public speaking when you are well prepared, and you radiate positive feelings to your audience so that their faces reflect these back to you. You might nod your head and smile to a few individuals before a speech, and when they nod back this will be a positive anchor for you just as your nodding was to them.

Happy and joyous people will have many positive anchors. When you feel good when reading, books become positive anchors. When you like more people, their names, pictures, and seeing them are positive anchors.

Make many positive anchors for yourself. When you are intensely in a positive state, such as joy, confidence, focused, or flowing, make a hand movement and/or sound. Every time you are in that state make the same hand movement or say the same words or sounds.

Some anchors last for years with only one experience. Other anchors need reinforcement. You have the ability to transform negative anchors into positive ones by intensely associating what used to be a negative anchor with something that is extremely positive. The power of anchors is so great that it makes sense to consciously master the ones that will enable you to be more joyous, more effective, and more helpful to others.

You can make new positive anchors for yourself with the sound of a telephone ringing, the beep of a horn, seeing a red or green light, knocking on a door, or even picking up a telephone to make a call. Let these and similar sounds and sights help you access your favorite states.

TODAY: THE GREATEST DAY OF YOUR LIFE

Today is the only day that you have. You have had previous days and hopefully, you will have many future days. But still today is the only day that you will experience in reality today. One way to transform today into a great day is to actually view it this way.

Some of the days that people consider the best days of their lives are because special events happened to them. But this is dependent on other people and external circumstances. You have the ability to develop yourself in ways that you can create your own greatest days.

Maimonides cites the story of a distinguished person who was asked, "What has been the most joyous day of your life?"

"It was a day that I was on a ship," he replied. "There were people on that ship who mocked and jeered me. They even threw garbage on me. My joy was that I was able to transcend this and create my own inner joy."

Yes, for this person this was a day of total liberation and freedom. He was now totally independent of external circumstances.

His happiness and joy were now totally dependent on his own mind. For him it was the greatest day of his life.

What would help you view today as the greatest day of your life? If today you have a greater awareness of your immense intrinsic value than ever before, then today is the greatest day of your life. If today you decide to upgrade your character beyond ways that you have done before, then today is the greatest day of your life. If today you make goals and plans that go beyond previous goals and plans, then today is the greatest day of your life. If today you have a greater spiritual awareness and feel more connected with the Creator than ever before, then today is the greatest day of your life.

The benefit of the previous ways of creating the greatest day of your life is that you can experience many days as your greatest days. Yesterday you reached your highest level up to that time of awareness of your intrinsic value and worth, but today your awareness is even greater. So yesterday was the greatest day until yesterday, but today you go even beyond that. And the same applies to character development, making goals and plans, and increased spiritual awareness and connecting with the Creator.

You can create a great day out of today by:
- *gaining greater self-mastery and self-discipline than ever before.*

- *learning something new and realizing that you know more today than ever before.*

- *forgiving someone you previously were not able to forgive.*

- *beginning a new habit that will make a great difference in your life.*

- *viewing your entire life until now in a new way that makes it more of a resource than ever before.*

- *doing something positive that you only now have the courage to do.*

- *upgrading your brain beyond any previous upgrade.*

- *embarking on a major learning program.*

38

THE MUSIC OF UPBEAT WORDS

Words are powerful. Like chemicals they change your body's inner chemistry. Happy people use happiness-producing words. When they are already in a joyous state, it is their automatic pattern. And when they are not in their best states, their usage of these words improves their state. Be aware of the words that increase your happiness, and those that decrease it.

You have your favorite words. Keep adding to them by listening to other joyous people. When you hear something you like, add it to your everyday vocabulary. Eskimos have many words for snow since the exact condition of the snow is highly relevant for them. Hopefully, you will have even more words for your positive feelings.

"It's wonderful that…"
"I'm excited about…"
"I'm happy that…"
"One of the most amazing things about…"
"That was terrific."
"Great!"

"Magnificent."

"You really sound enthusiastic about that."

"Unbelievable."

"You put me in a great state when you said that."

"I'm thrilled that..."

"I felt like celebrating when I heard the wonderful news."

"I'm feeling better all the time." (Doesn't this sound better than, "I'm still not totally well.")

"That's a beautiful thought."

"Brilliant!"

"I witnessed an act of true kindness today."

"My most joyous moment so far today was when..."

"This reminds me of a great story..." (This sentence gives you an opportunity to retell all your great stories. Especially since you are now reading that, "Anything anyone says will remind you of your favorite stories." So you can say the sentence, "This reminds me of a great story," with a straight face.)

One last comment: When you speak about what you do not like, minimize the intensity of the words you use. For example, you might say, "I would have preferred that things were different." This is lighter than habitually using words like *terrible* and *awful* — with the exception of the sentence: "It's terrible and awful not to use upbeat words." But even here it is preferable to say, "It's wonderful, terrific, magnificent, and amazing to use the power of upbeat words."

39

MASTERING SELF-MASTERY

Having self-mastery over your impulses makes a person mighty and powerful (*Ethics of the Fathers* 4:1). This gives us many opportunities to feel joy for increased self-mastery. When a person feels deprived by not giving in to impulses, it makes it difficult to maintain self-discipline. But when you are able to feel joy for self-mastery, the process becomes easier and more enjoyable.

When someone shows extraordinary physical strength in one form or another, he feels proud of his accomplishment. But the accomplishment of self-mastery is even greater. For this is an ongoing challenge to overcome impulses. Look at each victory as building your spiritual muscles and cherish even small achievements.

Some common examples:

You would like to eat something that is not healthy for you to eat. Feel empowered for not eating it. The same applies to maintaining any form of diet that you are keeping for your welfare.

You have a strong craving for a cigarette, but realizing how dangerous it is to your health, you move your hand away from it. Feel intense joy that you made a choice for life.

You feel anger towards someone and would like to insult him.

Feel so much pleasure in having self-mastery that the pleasure of not saying the insult is greater than the pleasure of saying it.

You know a piece of gossip. You feel that you must share it with others. But you reflect on how wrong it is to spread such gossip and you talk about other subjects. Feel the pleasure of having this self-mastery.

Someone asks you if you could do them a favor. Normally, you would agree to do the favor for others. But this person often refuses to do you favors. You overcome your initial reaction to refuse and you do the favor for this person. Feel great joy that you are able to act according to elevated values and are able to transcend your original impulse.

You caused someone distress. And now you have an obligation to apologize. But this person often causes you distress. You would easily be able to apologize if this person were likewise to apologize to you. But without you taking the initiative, this person is unlikely to apologize to you. Be the powerful one and apologize, whether or not this person will be willing to reciprocate.

It is beneficial to keep a self-mastery journal. Write down each act of self-mastery. This will increase your motivation and will give you a clear view of your progress. Since it is natural to have counterproductive impulses, enjoying acts of self-discipline give you many opportunities for the joy of victory. Moreover, knowing that you have frequently been successful will give you the energy to keep going in case you do not succeed all the time. Knowing that you have had self-mastery before increases your confidence in your having self-mastery in the future.

40.

CELEBRATE VICTORIES

The most joyous people are those who celebrate major victories. Each day find personal victories you can celebrate. All over the planet people celebrate sports victories. Learn from this the human potential for celebration and keep finding new things to celebrate in your own life.

What is a sports victory? Someone made up a set of rules about how to play a certain game. Members of schools, cities, or countries compete with other teams. One team wins and another one loses. Those who score more points rejoice. They cheer, shout, and celebrate. The endorphin level in the blood goes up. Their faces radiate joy. Their voices are jubilant. You too can experience this regularly when you master the ability to rejoice and celebrate at will.

Don't we need an actual victory to celebrate? Yes and no. "Actual" victories are arbitrary. If you are not interested in a certain sport, even if your city's or country's team wins, you will find it inconsequential and will not feel excited at their victory. And you can decide this moment to act as if you were celebrating the greatest victory that ever was and shout, yell, and jump as if you were ecstatically enthusiastic and joyous. If you are good at doing this without any special external event, you are fortunate. You have a tool that will energize and empower you at will.

Make a list of your victories and keep celebrating them. Every achievement and success is a victory that you can cherish for a lifetime. Learning how to read was a victory. And so was learning how to write. Doing the difficult is a victory. And so is overcoming personal handicaps and limitations. Feeling joy for the joy of others is a victory, and so is acting in an elevating matter towards someone who does not interact with you the way he should. Transcending an insult is a victory and so is doing an act of kindness when you do not feel like doing it. Realizing that these acts of self-mastery are victories will fill your life with opportunities to rejoice. A victory that others cheer is easily recognizable as a victory. Feel your own inner celebration when only you know about your victory. This is more difficult than a public victory and therefore you have more to celebrate.

Some time during each day ask yourself, "What victory can I celebrate today?" At times it might be easy for you to find a victory. There might be days when it will take more creativity for you to find a victory. You might even have to go out of your way to do something special to create a new victory. And that is exactly why seeking victories to celebrate is so powerful.

41.
HAPPINESS: CLAIMING WHAT IS RIGHTFULLY YOURS

You have valid reasons for experiencing happiness. You are alive, you are breathing, your brain is functioning. If you are not happy right now (and you are not in mourning), then in one form or another your brain is limiting you emotionally. Use your imagination to enable you to be in the state that you ought to be in.

Here is an effective technique to create joy. Ask yourself: "In what situations or circumstances would I be happy?" Then imagine that this is your reality. "But how can I fool myself?" some ask. That is why we started with the first paragraph. Since you should be happy, if you are not, your brain is playing a trick on you. You will now use your imagination to cancel out this blockage.

So when would you be happy?

"I would be happy if I suddenly became wealthy." Imagine that you just acquired enormous wealth. Visualize this in detail. Now feel the joy that you would experience. Since the joy of being alive is greater than the joy of wealth, you have a right to do this. And you do have many other things to rejoice about.

"I would be joyous if I wrote a book that sold 50 million copies." Then imagine that you did. Hear the publisher telling you that you reached this milestone. Influencing a single individual should give you tremendous joy. Use your imagination to claim what is rightfully yours.

"I would be joyous if I were awarded a medal of honor in the presence of a hundred thousand people." Then do some positive act and visualize the great honors of receiving your medal with everyone you knew present. When you do a positive act, you are entitled to this joy even if no one else knows about your actions. Your imagination is making it easier for you to feel the way you should.

"I would be joyous if I were told I had a serious illness and then was told I had a miraculous recovery." Imagine the news of your good health ("Great news. You are healthy.") and appreciate the good health that is already yours. Even a person who is seriously ill can appreciate the news that he has a longer lease on life.

"I would be joyous if I took an I.Q. test and was told that I am a supergenius." Imagine this and experience joy. You have a right to feel this joy with the miraculous power of your brain even if there are other people with similar intelligence. Overcome your lack of appreciation for the abilities you do have, with your ability to imagine unlimited mental potential.

Some people will love this exercise. Others will find it odd. But remember that millions upon millions of people enjoy fictional stories in books and movies. What we are referring to here is using your imagination to experience valid and realistic joy. Permit yourself to use the unrealistic to learn to enjoy the realistic.

42

THE JOYOUS CIRCLE OF EXCELLENCE

Mentally create a large circle. Visualize this circle as a joyous space. Just imagining stepping into this circle will enable you to access a joyous state at will. After you are able to do this, you have a tool you can use whenever you want to experience joy and empowerment.

People have used the imagery of the circle of excellence for all forms of inner resources. You can create states of courage, humor, creativity, empowerment, flowing, being centered and balanced, and any other state you wish.

Now let us go a bit slower and build up this tool. Imagine a large circle. The color of the circle can be any color you want. It can be a circular line around green grass or an empty space. Step into this circle and imagine yourself being intensely joyous. Feel what you would feel if you knew your Father, your King, Creator and Sustainer of the universe, blessed you. See yourself with a radiant smile. Hear yourself talking with joyous enthusiasm. Allow yourself to feel how you would feel if you were intensely joyous.

Now step out of the circle and see more joy being added to that circle. Imagine yourself stepping back into that circle and experiencing joy as soon as you do. Every time you automatically experience happiness or joy, imagine yourself standing in the circle of joy. This will increase the potency of the circle.

You can do the same with any other inner resource you want to be able to access at will. Think of a skill you already have that you want to excel in. Now remember a specific instance when you excelled at doing that skill. Think the thoughts you had when you excelled. Remember your total physiology, your posture, the look on your face, the same muscle tension, the same breathing. Now think of a role model who is an expert in this area. Imagine that you are that person or that you had been given that person's expertise as a gift. Now intensify these feelings and thoughts. Whenever you want to access these strengths, step into your circle of excellence and feel yourself becoming more energized.

43

YOUR LIFE AS A GROWTH SEMINAR

W hen people go to workshops and seminars that will help them develop and grow, they are willing to try out all types of exercises and experiments. They consider it fun and enjoyable to do things that they have not done before and might even have experienced as distressful. But since it is being defined as part of the growth experience, they reframe it in a positive manner. In fact, the more difficult something is, the more you gain by trying it out.

When you view your entire life as a growth seminar and all that happens as just exercises and experiments, each experience teaches you something. You learn something from each reaction. You learn how to prepare yourself for similar things that might occur in the future. The difficult becomes fun. Even what is not that enjoyable is viewed in a positive light for it enriches you and adds depth.

At a growth seminar you view all the other people who attend the seminar with you as your partners in growth. Everything they say and do as part of the suggested exercises are designed to help you develop your character. Some people will confront you and point out faults and shortcomings. View this as a welcome opportunity to improve. Develop a sense of humor and enjoy the total experience.

Imagine someone coming over to you and criticizing you in ways that no one else has ever done. You might feel very offended, hurt, angry, or overwhelmed. But then the person says to you, "Here is a check for a million dollars. I was just giving you the exercise that precedes this gift." How will you now view that experience of being criticized? It will be something that will put you in a great state every time you talk about it. Growth and development are valuable commodities. So when everything that happens to you is viewed as part of the workshop or seminar that helps you grow, you will now realize the value of things that you might not have otherwise viewed as valuable as they actually are.

Think about past experiences that you did not exactly enjoy. Look back at those experiences and view them as part of your lifetime growth seminar. Keep learning new lessons and gain new strengths.

44.

THE RIGHT COACH

We each have our blind spots. I do, and so do you. A teacher or coach can point them out to us. It is easier to see the blind spots of others than our own.

At times we will be stuck. We need another person to pull us out of the rut or swamp. When we feel stuck, we do not have immediate access to all of our inner strengths. We are not in touch with our best moments. We might fail to see the entire picture. A coach or teacher can help us gain perspective. He can remind us that we have inner resources that are ours when we acknowledge them.

No matter how much you know, there will always be new knowledge and ideas that a perceptive and skillful coach can teach you. At times we just need to be reminded about something we have forgotten to apply in our present situation. Then someone we ourselves have taught can serve as our teacher.

Keep your eyes open. Teachers come in many forms. A joyous person, who maintains resourceful states when we do not, can be a teacher. And so can someone who is not so joyous, but finds it easy to tell you what he does not apply himself. A teacher might be a professional, or a young child who enjoys life. A teacher can be someone you see regularly, or someone you meet once in a while. A teacher can even be someone you encounter in passing for a minute or two.

Ask joyous people, "Who taught you to be happy?" When they answer, ask, "What were the specific attitudes, ideas, beliefs, and tools they taught you?" In answering, this person has become your teacher.

"But I can't find anyone to teach me," some people complain.

First of all, it is not that you *cannot*, just that you *have not yet*. Keep looking. It is worth the investment in time and energy. If one potential coach does not work out, try someone else. It could even be that someone whose ideas and approaches did not work for you one time can be helpful another time.

When you consult someone to increase your happiness, know what you want, and ask for it. It is common to ask for what one does not want. "I do not want to be depressed." "I do not want to be so miserable." This way you might end up speaking more about depression and misery than on mastering joy. You might need to discuss the roots and causes in order to change what can be changed. But keep your main focus on joy, happiness, and self-mastery. If this is what you really want, keep your focus on what you can do in thought and deed to create it.

When you report back to your coach or teacher, focus on what worked for you. Focus on progress and improvement. Then when you discuss what went wrong, you will do so with the outcome of joy in mind.

Some people say, "I don't want joy, I just don't want to be miserable." But I've never heard a truly joyous person say this. Ironically, it is easier to go for joy than to go for "not being unhappy." Joy, by its very essence, will render you "not unhappy." Neutrality, however, is not as powerful. So go for joy, the more intense the better.

Until you find a live and breathing coach, hopefully this book and others like it will be your teachers. When you view a book as your teacher, you will gain more from your reading experience.

45.

CHILDREN LEARN BY YOUR EXAMPLE

Our childhood creates the foundation upon which we build our lives. A child who is taught joy has an easier time to live a joyous life. With effort and guidance an adult can master joy even with an unhappy childhood. But parents owe it to their children and themselves to think, speak, and act in ways that create a joyous home atmosphere. Children with joyous parents will find it easier to be happier.

Your own emotional states will be taught by osmosis to your children. When you are joyous about life in general, and about the various tasks and jobs you do both in and out of the house, your children experience a positive role model on how to speak and act joyously. Each parent will have his or her own style. Be yourself, but be your joyous self.

The way you reframe happenings will create your children's reality. If a three-year-old spills milk when pouring it onto his cereal, do not reframe this as a tragedy and yell at your child. Rather, you can say, "There is no need to cry over spilled milk. It's wonderful how you are learning this skill. All mistakes are learning experiences. Be happy that now you know how to do it better than before."

When difficulties arise, keep saying, "This is an opportunity for us to learn something. Let's make the best of the situation."

See the good and positive in your children and praise them. Motivate with positive wording. When you want to motivate your children to do something, begin with statements such as, "You will gain a lot by doing this." Then show your child how specifically he or she will gain. "You will feel better when you act right." This way your children associate good deeds with good feelings.

Even when children need to be disciplined, speak as calmly as possible. Prepare yourself for times of frustration and anger. Positive ways of expressing yourself should be so internalized that even when you are not in a calm state, the way you express yourself will be basically positive. For example, "I care about you, so I feel bad if you do anything harmful to yourself or your brothers and sisters." "You are precious to me so I sometimes get angry when you do something dangerous."

Your tone of voice when speaking to your children sets the tone for their way of speaking, even when they speak to themselves. If you have an abrasive way of speaking to them, practice speaking pleasantly. Professional singers spend countless hours practicing for their audiences. All parents are professional communicators and all children are entitled to be spoken to pleasantly.

If you realize that you caused your children unwarranted pain and suffering, apologize. Your expressing your regret can be a powerful healing experience at any age.

Greet your children in a way that they will be able to say about you what someone told me, "What I love about my parents is that whenever I came home, they made me feel that they were as happy to see me as they would the most distinguished guest."

My life has been tragic. What destroyed any chance of happiness for me was my parents' constant criticism.

"We're only doing this for your good," they told me. Sure they were. I do not believe that they could be so stupid to think that a constant barrage of verbal attacks was going to make me into a better person.

"If you keep doing things like this," they shouted, "you will ruin your life." The words that I kept hearing were "keep doing things like this," and "ruin your life." I've learned that these are called "embedded commands." But whatever you want to call them, I hate them. These patterns gave me a miserable childhood, low self-esteem, and an unfortunate life. I realize that at my age, it is time to stop blaming my parents, and start doing what I can to make a happy life for myself. Oh, how I wish my parents would have spoken more positively to me. I understand that they both had critical parents, but they still should have done a better job.

No rational parent would want this to be their children's reaction towards them. Let your children be able to say, "Of course, joy comes easy to me. I had such wonderful parents."

46

BEYOND YOUR REACH

A happy person is one who experiences joy with what he does have. Even though he tries to accomplish more in order to obtain more of what he wants, he keeps his main focus on feeling appreciation for what he does have. Those who keep their main focus on what they do not have only create distress for themselves, especially if they focus on what is totally beyond their reach.

"But how do I know what is really beyond my reach?" some people ask. "Perhaps I might think that something is beyond my reach and it really isn't."

True. You can always strive to achieve and accomplish more. If you succeed, that is terrific. But if you find out that some things are beyond your reach, you have a choice to make. You can either feel pain that you did not reach what you would have liked to reach, or you can choose to feel pleasure because of all that you have achieved or acquired. Since it is the nature of life on our planet to always want more than we actually have, the first choice guarantees misery. The second choice, however, which is the sensible choice if your priority is to live a happy life, guarantees you pleasure from your accomplishments.

You might be focusing on some people who have done, accomplished, or acquired more than you. But it is very possible that those very same people are focusing on other people who have done, accomplished, and acquired more than they have. If you experience happiness with what is in your reach, you are really in much better shape than they are.

Here are some examples of ways we can learn not to focus on unrealistic goals:

You might deserve a raise, but if your boss refuses to give it to you, that is beyond your reach. Appreciate the money you do receive even while you make plans on how to earn more.

You might want to have a perfect memory for all that you study, but if you study efficiently and still forget, a perfect memory is beyond your reach. Feel appreciation for what you do remember.

You might want to write a book that will sell five million copies, but only a fraction of that amount will be sold. The books that were not sold are beyond your reach. Appreciate the number of people who actually read your book.

You might want everyone in the world to be your friend. But you realize that this unrealistic goal is beyond your reach. Appreciate the friends you do have.

You might want to be happy all the time. But life does not always unfold the way you would wish. And you have not yet mastered the skill of being happy, regardless of what is occurring. So being happy all the time is beyond your reach. Appreciate each moment that you are happy.

47

FLEXIBLE WISH LIST

Wouldn't it be wonderful if you could have all your wishes fulfilled? We assume that if a person's big wishes come true, then happiness will be a cinch. Not necessarily so. Even if a wish is fulfilled, it could be disappointing. I remember hearing a story about an entire city where everyone was blessed that one wish of theirs would be fulfilled. Most of the people wished to win the large city's lottery. And they all chose the winning number. Since the grand prize was going to be divided among all those who made the correct choice, they had to divide the large amount of money between a large amount of people. The actual amount won was therefore only a few dollars each.

A great Chassidic master once gave this formula for having your wishes met. "If things do not go the way you wish, wish them to go the way they are," advised Rabbi Mordechai of Lechovitz.

Spiritually, what is best for you is what is. Therefore if you were able to see all of reality, you would really wish for exactly what is best for you, which is your actual experiences.

Enjoy your wishes even before they come true. Then you can

enjoy the pleasant thoughts of how happy you will be if those wishes become reality. And if those wishes do not become your reality, immediately start wishing that things should be the way they are.

Mastering the skill of wishing for what is takes practice. If you grew up with this consciousness as a young child, it will be easy for you. You will even wonder why anyone would not do it. There is much to gain and nothing to lose. But if you did not grow up with this approach to wishes, wish for yourself to master it. This is one of the ultimate wishes that you can wish for.

48

SEEKING SOLUTIONS

Become a solution-seeker. When a problem arises, ask yourself, "What solution can I think of?" When a situation is not to your liking, ask yourself, "What solution can I think of?" Whenever something is bothering you, ask yourself, "What solution can I think of?"

Unhappy people become distraught, upset, frustrated, or angry when unpleasant things happen. They speak to themselves and to others in ways that increase the amount of time they will feel emotional distress.

Happy people use their intelligence and memory to think of potential solutions. At times solutions might be easy to find if you just ask yourself, "What solution can I think of?" If a solution is not easy to find, brainstorm in your own mind or with others.

Be creative when you try to think of solutions. Some ideas you come up with might be impractical. But by thinking in the right direction, you will find a solution.

When you cannot come up with a total solution, ask yourself, "What can I do to improve upon things?" You might be able to think of ways to make the situation easier to cope with. Or you might be able to compensate for your loss.

You just lost your job. This easily causes much stress. Think about different ways you can now earn money. You might find a better job. You might start a business that makes you wealthy. Or you might find things you can do temporarily until you find a job that you really like.

Your electronic organizer just broke. Your immediate reaction is panic. "Oh, no, what will I do without it?" you hear yourself saying. Think of ways to access your most important and frequently used telephone numbers. You might find this easier to do than you initially imagined.

If someone consistently speaks to you in a way that causes you distress, think of a potential solution. Perhaps you can find communication patterns that will influence this person to speak to you more pleasantly or respectfully. Perhaps you can learn patterns of thought and mental exercises to make you immune to the inappropriate patterns of others. If you cannot come up with a plan yourself, consult an expert who can advise you.

You have to learn some new information or a skill that you find overwhelming. You are beginning to feel totally discouraged and are ready to give up. Think of someone who might be able to help you master the material or the skill. Everyone can learn everything if it is presented and taught to them the right way. Search for someone who can do this for you.

49

CHILDREN OF ROYALTY

I would like to share a story that I heard from a parent who had a large family. This parent would complain that his children were very difficult to handle. I had not seen him in quite a while, but recently we bumped into each other. Unlike the past, he was now full of appreciation and praise for his children. I asked him what had made the difference. And this is what he told me:

"I hated to admit it, but I was having a difficult time accepting my children. I resented the amount of time and effort that I had to spend disciplining them. I found myself becoming angry with them over trivialities. I tried various approaches and techniques, but nothing worked for me for very long.

"My own parents were not always patient with me. And I, in turn, lacked patience for my children. I was afraid that I would be guilty of passing this on to my grandchildren.

"It was suggested to me, 'Try for one full week to view your children as children of the Creator. They are special and precious. The Creator and Sustainer of the universe believed in you and gave you His children to watch and to guide, to love and to care for. Treat them as you know He would want you to care for them.'

"This concept immediately appealed to me. I remembered a time when early in my marriage, a very distinguished neighbor asked us to look after his children for a couple of hours. I looked on it as a great privilege. I spoke to those children as if they were members of royalty. I resolved to do the same for my own children.

"When I first heard about the idea I thought that it would be beneficial, but the actual results amazed me. I realized that I had been getting frustrated and angry because I felt my children were wasting my time. Now I realized that the One Who gave me time was telling me to use it to raise our children, His and mine, with patience and love.

"I no longer feel that I have a right to get angry with my children for not listening to me as quickly as I would have wanted. My Creator, Whose children they ultimately are, wants me to transform anger into patience and frustration into understanding. I need to teach and coach, but always with love and with an understanding of the unique nature of each child.

"During the last six months, the entire atmosphere in our home has changed dramatically. I have gained a much greater appreciation for my children. I now try to see situations from my children's point of view. This has opened my eyes to an entirely new world. It has given me much greater understanding of who my children are and why they act the way they do from their point of view.

"My patience and love have had a positive effect on their personalities. Both the content of what I say and my tone of voice have influenced my children to follow my requests and suggestions in ways that I would not have believed possible in the past. This in turn makes it even easier for me to treat them the way children of the Creator should be treated."

50

LASTING FREEDOM

I t was a few days before the holiday of Passover. I was sitting in the barber's chair getting a haircut as part of my pre-Passover preparations. All of a sudden there was a power failure and the lights went out.

"There goes the electricity again," one customer exclaimed. "Isn't it awful how these things keep happening!"

"Now we can appreciate the electricity even more when it comes on again," I consoled him.

Then I thought of how this was an appropriate preparation of attitude for the upcoming holiday. We were going to celebrate freedom from slavery. Freedom is precious. But when you have lived with freedom your entire life, you sort of take it for granted. We should not. Appreciating freedom adds an important dimension to each day of our lives. Some people have major issues with boredom. Yes, boredom can be very painful. But a slave who is forced to work until total exhaustion overtakes him is not bored. And he would gladly trade places with someone who is. A person who has freedom can creatively find many solutions to the problem of boredom.

I made a commitment that from then on, every time I would experience an electricity failure, I would immediately think, "Now I am going to appreciate the fact that I have freedom." Instead of feeling frustrated for what was not going right, I would use what happened to remind myself to be more grateful.

After writing this down, the thought came to me, "I don't need to limit this just to the lights going out. I can apply this pattern in many ways." And so can you. Whenever something distressful happens, besides finding a solution, let it remind you to think of what you can be appreciative of in your life.

Brains function like data bases. When something distressful happens, it is easy for your brain to think of other distressful memories. But you have the ability to channel your brain's associations to a more joyful path. Mentally connect minor frustrations to remind you to be grateful for what is positive in your life. For example, if something falls from your hand, you can immediately exclaim, "Fantastic, gravity is still working for us." Or, if your computer does not work as you want it to, you can react, "I'm grateful for my eyesight that lets me see what is happening."

51

ADD A HAPPY ENDING TO YOUR WORRIES

Worry has proved to be one of the main ways people rob themselves of happiness. A happy mind is a mind free of worry, while a worried mind is certainly not very happy. No happiness is so great that it can withstand the vicious onslaught of worry. There is a valuable formula for getting rid of all your worries, but before we get rid of worry, we need to define it.

Worry is when you fantasize unhappy endings and these endings cause you distressful feelings. A worrier thinks of what might possibly go wrong and feels anxiety before anything bad actually happens. Worry means you are paying the price for trouble that has not even occurred and which may not even happen. If things go wrong, a non-worrier can enjoy life until then. Why hurry with your worry?

The wise thing to do is to plan ahead and to take precautionary measures to prevent problems whenever and wherever such actions are possible. Since worry is based on fantasy, use fantasy for your benefit. Develop the ability to fantasize happy endings. "But what if something does not have a happy ending?" you might ask. The non-worrier's response is: First of all, why suffer when events might not turn out as badly as you fantasized? Second, you might actually cope better than you thought you would with a reality that is not to your liking. Third, since you are making a choice of your fantasies about the future, choose enjoyable ones instead of those that are needlessly distressing.

One person who tried this out told me, "I cannot believe that overcoming worry was so simple. I have been a worrier for years. I suffered immensely about all kinds of worries and the vast majority of things I worried about did not take place. When I first heard about mentally visualizing happy endings, I thought it was ridiculous. I am a realist and do not want to live in a fantasy world. Then I realized that no worrier lives in the real world. The fantasies might seem realistic, but by definition, they are not.

"I started visualizing happy endings. Of course, not everything turns out as positively as I imagine. But I enjoy my imaginary scenarios and I cope better with actual problems and difficulties. I now use my creative imagination to figure out the best way to handle whatever happens. I highly recommend the 'happy ending technique' to all worriers. And if they try it out and still prefer worrying, at least it's now a deliberate choice."

52.

BE HAPPY FOR WHAT DID NOT HAPPEN

When people think about happiness, they usually think about being happy for positive things that occur. Rabbi Simcha Zissel of Kelm (1824-1898) wrote to his students to appreciate what did not happen. He commented on a puzzling custom that he saw. When a shirt would fall from a clothesline into the dirt, some people would say, "I am grateful that I was not in that shirt." It sort of makes you want to smile, does not it?

He explained that people play games and listen to music in order to enjoy life. Developing the habit of being grateful for all the wrong things that did not occur in your life will add to your daily dose of enjoyment.

When you learn to appreciate what did not happen, it's mind-boggling how many bad things do not happen to you in one day. I have told some people to make a daily list of ten bad things that did not happen to them. Some find this unpleasant. And for them there are other paths to appreciation. But for those who find this beneficial here are some examples that people have listed.

- *Today, I did not lose all of my possessions.*

- *Today, I was not stranded on an isolated deserted island.*

- *Today, I did not lose my five senses.*

- *Today, our planet did not explode.*

- *Today, my parachute did not fail to open when I jumped out of an airplane. (If you never jumped out of an airplane, you can still enjoy this thought.)*

- *Today, I did not get on the wrong plane and wind up lost in a foreign country.*

- *Today, I did not wake up with the data base of my brain totally empty of all memories and knowledge.*

- *Today, the sun did not burn itself out.*

- *Today, there are many illnesses and injuries from which I did not suffer.*

- *Today, I was not hit by lightning.*

- *And for those who find this exercise unpleasant:*
  "Today I did not make a list of unpleasant things that did not happen to me."

53

COLLECTING PICTURES

Keep a scrapbook of pictures that you can enjoy looking at over and over again. You can find them in advertisements, in travel brochures, in magazines that are about to be thrown out. My favorite is collecting pictures of people smiling, rejoicing, or laughing. Every time you look at hundreds of people smiling, you will find it easy to smile yourself. Some people prefer to organize their picture collections into subjects. Others prefer to store them randomly. Here are some of the subjects you can collect:

- *Snapshots of friends*
- *Waterfalls*
- *Trees and forests*
- *Flowers and gardens*
- *Mountains*
- *Jungles*
- *Great people*
- *Lakes, ponds, and oceans*

- *Places you have visited*
- *Places you would like to visit and historical sites*
- *Wild animals, such as lions, elephants, bears, monkeys*
- *Domestic animals, such as dogs and cats*
- *Birds and butterflies*
- *Fish of various shapes and colors*
- *Interesting advertisements*
- *Action-oriented pictures or people successfully doing dangerous things, such as climbing mountains, hanging onto beams to fix something high in the air, riding a wild bronco*
- *Countrysides*
- *Great architecture*
- *Beautiful homes and furniture*
- *Great paintings*
- *Large crowds and parades*
- *Snow*
- *Deserts*
- *Historic scenes*
- *Insightful cartoons*
- *Other planets, stars, and galaxies*
- *People playing musical instruments (You can then mentally hear them playing.)*

54

IT IS ALL IN YOUR IMAGINATION

What is the difference between the imagery of happy people and those who have not yet mastered happiness?

Answering this question will enable you to create positive imagery. As you gain greater control over the pictures you visualize in your brain, you will be able to intensify the enjoyable ones and lessen the effects of distressful ones.

Picture a car of any type or color. Now, let it go and picture an orange. It might be on a tree, on a plate in your kitchen, or in your hand. You might even be eating it and can smell and taste it now. Now, let it go and picture the car you saw before. Now, picture an elephant. Your elephant could be in a zoo or in a jungle, standing still or running. If you were able to move from a car to an elephant it means you can control your mental pictures.

Now take your mental car and make it bright yellow. Make the picture very large and also close to you. After you do this, change the color to a dull gray and make the picture small and far away. Notice any differences you feel towards the car with the different submodalities (the Neurolinguistic Programming — NLP — term for these changes).

When you are able to do this, you have experienced the skill that will enable you to create joyous mental images. Keep replaying your most joyous memories. Remember them in vivid detail. You can also create new mental pictures of events that have not yet happened. Even if the probability is less than slight that the event will actually occur, you can still utilize it to create enjoyable states. You can also visualize relaxing and pleasant scenes, either those that you already experienced or those you mentally create. And make it a habit to visualize yourself succeeding at what you wish to do.

The principle to remember is: Make the joyous pictures you want to intensify large and colorful. Make them big and close. You can even add your favorite music and add any details to the scene that will enhance it for you.

If you needlessly visualize distressful scenes, you have a few choices. Either change mental channels and run more pleasant and enjoyable scenes. Or, you can make the unpleasant scenes tiny and move them far away into the distance. Have them fly to the sun and melt away. Transform details to change the emotional effect.

Some people find this easy to do. Even if at first you find that this takes a lot of effort, keep practicing. This is a skill that will increase your positive feelings and decrease negative ones. If you are running mental movies, it makes sense to run the kind that enhance the quality of your life.

55

PRE-SLEEP CONDITIONING

Right before you go to sleep, your brain enters an altered state that is conducive for conditioning it to increase happiness. As you give your brain happiness-producing messages when you are in a relaxed state, those messages become a part of your daily thinking. Add mental pictures of yourself being happy and the effect is stronger. At the same time you will be programming your unconscious to produce happier dreams. Read this mental program before you go to sleep for at least a month. Be patient and persistent and you will experience the benefits.

Now, you are about to become more and more relaxed, as you begin to let go of all stress and tension. As you continue to breathe, you are becoming more and more relaxed with each and every breath. Any noise that you hear is making you even more and more relaxed and sleepy. You are more and more open to create a more joyous way of being and are creating more potential for happiness for yourself and others.

Now, allow yourself to visualize a relaxing and peaceful scene. See a beautiful garden, with colorful flowers and comfortable weather. Hear calm and soothing music that will make you more and more relaxed. See and feel yourself becoming more and more relaxed as you hear a soft and gentle voice telling you, "You are becoming more and more relaxed with each breath. And this will make you more and more open to create happiness each and every day."

As you keep breathing, begin to see a wonderful smile on your face. The part of you that creates dreams will show you that you are more and more appreciative and grateful for all that you can appreciate. See yourself talking and acting with more and more joy. Happiness and joy will become so much a part of your nature that you will automatically and spontaneously feel this way.

As you see yourself as being happy and joyous, see yourself being this way tomorrow and each and every day after that. Each and every breath makes this more and more your natural reality.

Now, hear yourself talking to yourself in ways that make you an even happier person than ever before. Allow yourself to hear positive empowering messages. Hear the voices of joyous people who care about you. Quiet any negative inner chatter and hear the type of messages that you need the most to live the best life you can possibly live.

Now, see yourself becoming an expert at finding positive ways of looking at things. Find the benefits and gains in every experience and situation. Begin to find humor where you had not seen it before.

Tomorrow you will easily think of more ways that you can bring more happiness to other people. Speak to others in ways that bring out their best. See yourself smiling to others and see others smiling back to you. You are becoming more and more cheerful and this benefits both yourself and others.

Keep hearing the most relaxing sounds and voices, and see the most relaxing pictures and scenes. These calm and relaxed feelings right now will let you sleep soundly and deeply and see and hear yourself becoming happier and happier. When you wake up you will find yourself with greater appreciation for the new day and new energy. Now allow yourself to become sleepier and sleepier so you will sleep peacefully and deeply until you wake up at the appropriate time refreshed and energized.

56

COMPLETING SENTENCES

The ideas in this sentence-completion exercise are conducive for accessing happiness-producing states. Over time you might find that your answers will change and this will give you insights into yourself.

- *I am committed to living a happy life because…*
- *What I am grateful for is…*
- *I talk and act joyously when…*
- *What I most appreciate about my father is…*
- *What I most appreciate about my mother is…*
- *The thoughts that create happiness for me are…*
- *My best friends…*
- *One of the greatest people I ever met was…*
- *For me the most relaxing scene is…*
- *One of the best trips I ever took was…*
- *My favorite music is…*
- *The nicest thing anyone ever said to me is…*

- *My most joyous memories are…*
- *When I was a child I was excited about…*
- *I am enthusiastic about…*
- *I will increase…*
- *The people who add to my happiness are…*
- *The way that I can add to the happiness of others is…*
- *What I can do to increase my happiness is…*
- *A kind action I can do is…*
- *I will learn more from…*
- *I felt joy for the joy of someone else when…*
- *I will now find a more positive way to look at…*
- *I felt happiest yesterday when…*
- *I feel a sense of accomplishment when…*
- *I feel motivated when…*
- *The type of humor that I like is…*
- *I feel fortunate that…*
- *What makes me smile is…*
- *One of my favorite dreams was…*
- *A story that gives me good feelings is…*
- *When I am in a positive state, I…*
- *What I have taken for granted, but will now appreciate more is…*
- *I pleasantly surprised myself when…*
- *I will bring more happiness to…*

57

THINKING BIG

I was redialing a busy phone number on a public telephone. As I waited a minute, I heard someone who was walking by say to two friends of his, "THINK BIG!" I have no idea what he was referring to, but for me this was an important message. And now that you are reading this, that passing remark is an important message for you and for anyone else that you influence with it.

What if a few times a day you would be greeted with a cheerful "THINK BIG"? This would be a constant reminder for your brain to think bigger than before. Exactly what this would mean to you would depend on where you are right at the moment when you hear or read these words.

As you are reading this book, thinking big might mean that you now decide that you are going to create a joyous and happy life for yourself beyond what you once thought possible. Thinking big might mean that you increase the size of your goals. Thinking big might mean that you were ready to give up and now your thinking big empowers you to keep going. Thinking big might mean that you decide to increase a donation to a worthwhile cause.

Thinking big might mean that you decide to let go of anger or resentment and forgive. Thinking big might mean that you do acts of kindness when it is difficult for you to do so. There are many ways to think big, as you will find out yourself when you continually THINK BIG!

Since we cannot expect complete strangers to keep reminding us to think big, it would be wise for you to repeat this message to yourself a few times a day. Some people keep a sign saying THINK BIG! in a place where they frequently see it.

It is possible for someone to think big and therefore be disappointed with small gains and benefits. But since that would cause disappointment and distressful feelings, ultimately this would be considered thinking little. Part of thinking big is to derive pleasure and joy from even small gains. At the same time, each small gain gives you a vision of ever larger gains and benefits.

As you think big, you will be able to view the entire planet as your resource for creating personalized inner resources. Some people will directly tell you information and ideas. They will consciously say things to inspire and motivate you. When you think big and view the entire world as your resource, anything anyone says about any topic or subject can be utilized by you as a source of inspiration and a reminder for you to continually upgrade your brain and your character.

Keep your eyes and ears open for opportunities to model great people. That is the ultimate way to think big. You will be adding the big thinking of others to your own big thinking. These can be people living anywhere on our planet right now. It could be people you have heard about who lived a long time ago. Whenever you read about anyone who was a big thinker, you now have an addition to your model of what it means to think big.

If you were totally motivated to think big, what one thing would you decide to think big about?

58

INCREASING ENERGY

A happy person has positive energy. In moments of intense joy, your energy level rises. Depression, on the other hand, is a depletion of energy. By increasing your level of energy, you will live a happier life.

Take care of your health. Eat well. Get enough sleep. Exercise regularly. Learn healthy ways to release stress and tension. Do not do things that needlessly drain you of your energy. Eating unhealthy food, lack of sleep, not exercising, negative thinking, all cause lack of energy.

Your thoughts can increase or decrease your level of energy. Being involved in something you find boring and meaningless saps energy. But the moment you think of something exciting, a creative idea, a way to make a major breakthrough, or anything similar, your energy level will immediately rise.

Imagine someone who is bored and tired. His only thoughts are that he would like to take a nap. Then he hears that he won the national lottery. In a fraction of a second, the energy level goes from low to high. The lottery might have been won the day before, but the moment he hears about it, it greatly effects his energy level.

You, like everyone else, will find that some people increase your energy level and some people decrease it. When possible, spend more time around those who create healthy energy for you. And when by necessity you are in the presence of people who do the opposite, do what you can mentally and verbally to create more positive energy.

Releasing stress and tension is crucial for those who wish to maintain healthy energy. At times, this might be complex. But often practicing relaxing slow breathing together with calming words such as, "Deeper and deeper relaxed with each breath," can decrease your degree of stress which will enable you to increase positive energy.

Be aware of anything that might be blocking your energy and be committed to remove these blocks. Holding on to painful past memories, envy, resentment, and anger deplete your energy in the present. For your own health and emotional welfare do what you can to let go. At times someone might need the help of a professional to do so.

Prayer can be one of the most effective energy builders. In your own words ask the All-powerful to renew your energy. By getting in touch with the Source of all energy, you will be increasing your own.

59

BRING HAPPINESS TO ONE PERSON EACH DAY

"You are so busy doing things for others. Do not you miss out a lot by not spending more time on yourself?"

This was a question an interviewer asked a person who ran a charitable organization.

"Just the opposite," he replied. "When I do for others I am really doing for myself. I might seem to others to be unselfish, but I know myself that I am very selfish. I feel so good when I do acts of kindness for others that I do not want to miss out on this pleasure."

You too can develop this unselfish selfishness. (Or is it selfish unselfishness?) Each and every day do at least one act of kindness for another person. You might want to try this out at times by doing a kind act for someone and that person will not even know about it. At other times, the person you help will be happy to know that you care.

What if you are alone and cannot find anyone for whom to do an act of kindness? Then write a letter. Or keep a list of some kind actions you can do as soon as you get an opportunity to. But there will usually be someone you can be kind to. There will be someone who will appreciate your praise or kind words.

After doing this daily, you might enjoy it so much that you will decide to do it many times a day. It is a fantastic way to increase your own happiness in a way that enhances the life of other people.

I was feeling depressed for a few months and finally decided to speak to a doctor about getting medication. The doctor told me that if medication was needed, he would give me a prescription. But he would suggest that I try out an approach that Dr. Alfred Adler, a pioneer in the field of psychoanalysis, often used with patients.

"If it works, I'll try it out," I said to him.

"For two weeks go out of your way to do a major act of kindness for someone who could use it."

"That sounds like something a clergyman would suggest. I'm surprised that you as a doctor are telling me to do this," I commented.

"Like you said yourself, 'If it works, I'll try it out.' This has worked for many people and I think it could work for you," he said with a kindly smile.

That was over a year ago and I never did need the medication. I felt great about myself as I became a kinder person. The gratitude and appreciation that I received were a real emotional lift. But even when what I did was not commented on, I felt wonderful. I feel like a new person and it was my own actions that created it.

60.

LISTENING TO OTHER PEOPLE'S LIFE STORIES

People love to talk about themselves. Each person is their own favorite subject. Some people are more open about this, others less so. But the need to be listened to and understood nonjudgmentally is a universal need. Telling our life story to someone who is sincerely interested in knowing who we really are is a wonderful experience. Listening to someone tell their life story can be a great act of kindness. This is especially so when you comment in ways that validate the other person's individuality and deep feelings.

When you enjoy listening to people tell about their lives, you have found a way to enjoy yourself in a way that greatly benefits others. Your listening attentively is especially valuable for the elderly, the lonely, the misunderstood, and people who are taken for granted. In some instances, your listening can be a lifesaver. Go out of your way to listen to those who are not usually listened to.

The form of listening referred to is not passive. It is an action. Listen with your total focus, your entire mind. When you listen, nothing else exists except the individual who is speaking. Listen as you would if you were a professional interviewer who will be paid a large sum of money for this interview. Listen as you would if this were the most fascinating human being you have ever met. Listen as you would if you were to know that this person would reveal to you some secrets about living that would transform your life. You can never know, perhaps someone will. And you might be transforming this person's life.

Learn from good listeners. A good listener leans forward and nods his head when a point is made. A good listener makes non-intrusive comments. These can be wordless sounds that express understanding and acceptance. Or they could be utterances no more profound than, "Yes," "I understand," "That's really something," "I know," "That must have been painful," "'Wow!" "Wonderful." "I'm sorry to hear that." "I hope that this gets better." Whenever you interact with a good listener, or observe one listening to someone else, see and hear what you can add to your own listening repertoire.

Good listeners are often considered great communicators. They make the person they listen to feel important. A truly good listener knows that every individual is an entire world and has intrinsic worth. Every individual is important. A person who lacks this view is less of an important person himself. As the Sages (*Ethics of the Fathers* 4:1) say, "Who is an honorable person? The one who honors others." And listening to people is a lofty form of honoring them. Not honoring others lowers the honor of the one who fails to give the honor.

I was shy and timid and wanted to become a better communicator. Someone told me, "Read interesting stories and articles and share them with others." I did this and found this helped to some degree. But what made a real difference in my life was the realization that my top priority as a communicator is to become a good listener. I read a number of interviews conducted by professional interviewers. I saw the patterns of the questions they asked and practiced asking these type of questions. I am amazed at how this has enhanced my life. Here are some of the patterns that I learned and used:

- *"What did you learn from that experience?"*

- *"What is most important to you about that?"*

- *"If you could do it differently now, what would you do?"*

- *"Have you ever done something similar?"*

- *"What are similar things that happened to you?"*

- *"How did you know to do it that way?"*

- *"Why do you think you had this reaction?"*

- *"What did this remind you of?"*

- *"What has made the biggest difference in your life?"*

- *"If I were interested in knowing how to do that, what*

would be most important for me to know?"

- *"How can you now look at this situation differently than when it first happened?"*

- *"What attributes did this help you develop?"*

- *"What exactly did you find challenging about that?"*

- *"How do you think the other person felt?"*

- *"In what ways did things turn out better than you thought they would?"*

- *"Why did you make that choice?"*

- *"What do you consider the best part of that for you?"*

- *"What was special about that?"*

- *"What have been the highlights of your life?"*

- *"What are your most cherished memories?"*

- *"Can you pinpoint the aspects that were most meaningful to you?"*

- *"Can you tell me more about that?"*

61

BRINGING OUT THE BEST IN OTHERS

"I would be very happy if there were not so many people who make me unhappy," the frustrated storekeeper said to me. "I have enough money to live a comfortable life. But the hassles that others cause me prevent me from enjoying my life."

"But you would not choose to live in solitary confinement," I pointed out.

"Of course not," he said, "but I cannot stand the way people treat me. It's not only the customers who ask me stupid questions and who waste my time without purchasing anything. Throughout the day, I meet people who are rude and inconsiderate."

"When you are with your family is it any better?" I asked.

"It's just as bad," he said sadly. "My children fight a lot with each other and do not listen to me. My wife is a wonderful person but we argue a lot. When I visit my parents, the first hour or so is pleasant, but it's always just a matter of time until I say things I'm sorry I said."

What was the essence of this person's difficulties? He was an expert at bringing out the worst in other people. He only noticed how he did not like the way others spoke to him. He forgot to focus on how he spoke to others. He was impatient. His tone of voice gave a message, "Leave me alone already. I cannot be bothered with you." The content of what he said was invariably critical. He, like others who experience people as he does, can change the way others treat him by changing the way he treats them.

When you speak to other people with sincere respect and sensitivity, you tend to bring out their best. See the good in other people. Even if you notice that they have faults, identify them with their strengths and positive qualities. When you radiate cheerfulness and good wishes to others, most people reciprocate. Not only will you be spared hassles and arguments, but you will be on the receiving end of the cheerfulness and good wishes of others. This will definitely add to your own happiness in life.

THE VISION OF A "GOOD EYE"

Other people will either be a resource for creating greater happiness in your life, or a source of distress and difficulties. Definitely, the nature and behavior of others is beyond your total control. But the way that you perceive other people will be a key element in making more people a resource or turning them into problems and adversaries.

It has been said, "You can tell more about a person by what he says about others than you can by what others say about him." As regards happiness, we can say similarly, "You can gain more happiness by what you say about other people than by what others say about you." And the way to speak positively about others is to see them in a positive light.

Every human being has positive qualities and faults. When someone does a good deed, you can either appreciate it or find something wrong. "Why did he take so long to do it?" "Why didn't he do even more?" "How come he did this and not this other thing which I consider more important?" A "good eye" sees the good that others do and gives generous praise and acknowledgment. People feel better about themselves when they are in the presence of such a person.

The person with a "bad eye" blames and complains a lot. This robs the person himself of good feelings and will lead to his saying things that can easily cause a negative loop. Negative statements boomerang and come back to cause problems for the speaker.

Try this exercise: Visualize an imaginary person and praise him with as many praises as you can think of for three minutes. Now think of an imaginary person and say as many negative things as you can think of for three minutes. Feel the difference in your own energy as you do this exercise. Praise and positive statements create healthy energy for you, the speaker, besides spreading good will and good feelings.

The world of the person with a "good eye" is clearer and more beautiful. It is a world that will enhance the life of the owner of those eyes and all the many people who will gain by being seen by those eyes.

"You can use my story to help others," he told me. "I used to feel that it was a greater sign of intelligence to see what was wrong with people and to notice their faults and weaknesses. I felt it was naïve and simplistic to just see the good. So I became an expert at cynicism and seeing faults. I felt that my way of seeing people was superior and more honest.

"But then I had a number of setbacks. My wife filed for divorce. 'I always feel put down in your presence,' she claimed. After the divorce my children hardly came to visit me. 'All he does is tell us what's wrong with us,' they told the social worker.

"After the divorce, my business was not going well. Key employees quit and we lost many accounts. I asked some employees for honest feedback, but I could see that most were hesitant to tell me what they really thought. Finally, one older fellow was straight with me.

"'People have always felt that you look down at them,' he said to me. 'But before your divorce you had more energy and drive. You paid well so people stayed with your company. But since your divorce, you've been tougher to deal with. You lost a lot of your energy and seem depressed a good part of the time. Your negativity has been more difficult to take.'

"I consulted a counselor to see what I could do to improve the situation. He told me that I had to make a choice. Either I keep seeing the negative in others and create more misery for myself. Or, I could start seeing the positive and the good in others. This would take considerable effort since I was so used to seeing the negative. But I would eventually reestablish a relationship with my children and build up my business. While working on this, I saw that I felt so much better about myself. My general emotional state improved a lot. And the only negative aspect was that I felt a lot of pain that I had not developed a good eye years before."

63

THE JOY FOR THE JOY OF OTHERS

"**O**ur team won!" is the jubilant victory cheer. "We won! We won!" total strangers will call out to each other. What happened? The sports team of their city has scored more points than another team sponsored by a different city.

This joy can last for many years. It is over 40 years since my home team, the Baltimore Colts (which no longer exist), won the "World Championship" (pre-Super Bowl era) in 1958. But whenever I recall that 23 to 17 victory, I once again experience a joyous moment of my youth.

Envy hurts. It destroys happiness and causes much suffering. Someone whose brain has subscribed to this attribute will always be able to feel miserable regardless of how much he or she has and how well life is going. Not everyone will tell you how much they suffer from envy, but most people do, some more intensely and some with mere tinges of pain.

What is the ultimate solution to envy? Learning to develop the attribute of experiencing joy as a result of the success of others. "But isn't that a very high spiritual level?" is the common reaction. "Does not it take a long time to be able to do this?" The answer can be found in the joy of those who root for the winning team. Since the fans identify with the winners, it is easy for them to be joyous because of the success of others even though they have never personally met them.

Root for the success of people you know as well as for people you do not know. (That about covers it for the people on our planet.) Whenever someone is successful in some endeavor, root for him and cheer. If this does not come naturally to you, you are not alone. The first reaction of many people is that this sounds impossible. But I can testify that it is a learnable skill if you practice.

How do you practice? Bill Gates's fortune has increased? Cheer for him. You see the announcement of an engagement, cheer for the happy couple. Someone wins an award for anything: Cheer! Someone wins a lottery: Cheer for the winner. Someone has achieved scholastically, created a new invention, has written another book, composed a new song: Cheer!

"Why should I do this?" some readers might ask.

"Because it feels great to be joyous and this is one of the best ways to consistently experience joy," is the answer.

From now on, be more aware of the choices you will be making throughout your life whenever you hear about someone's success. You can choose to be envious. This choice gives you nothing but pain. Or you can choose to be neutral. With this choice you do not suffer, but you miss out on a lot of life's potential for joy. Or you can choose to experience joy because of the joy of others. With this choice, you will have unlimited opportunities to experience joy. A wise choice, isn't it?

64

BRING SMILES TO OUR PLANET

"I love it when people smile at me," I heard him say. "So I do the one thing that will guarantee my receiving a lot of smiles from many people."

"What is that?" the listener asked. "Hardly anyone ever smiles at me. As a matter of fact, that is one of my biggest complaints against other people. They do not smile enough. As soon as I see that someone's does not smile at me, I feel so bad about it that my entire emotional state drops rapidly."

"When I tell you what you have to do, you might laugh or discount it," the first speaker continued. "It's so simple that an infant can do it, and many of them do. Smile at each person you encounter. Sometimes it will be appropriate to add a friendly greeting. But even when you do not say anything verbally, the positive message of a nonverbal smile says a lot more than words."

I could not tell whether the listener would actually put this into practice, but anyone who does will find that even complete strangers tend to smile back. Try it yourself. If you are apprehensive about this, then just smile slightly and nod your head just a bit.

Imagine how wonderful our planet would be if each person on it would greet everyone with a smile. That means that wherever you go you would be met with a smile. Be part of the "Bring a smile to our planet" project. To become a member of this project, you do not need to spend any money or fill out any forms. All you need to do is smile. Then watch the faces of those at whom you smile. Reinforce the smiles of others by telling them, "I appreciate your smiles," or, "You look great when you smile." By reinforcing this person's smiling, you will set in motion a chain of smiles. The recipients of this person's smiles will smile to more people, and those people will smile to even more people. You will be increasing the total amount of smiles on our planet. And that is something we need a lot more of.

Think of someone who does not smile very often. Then sensitively think of a way to bring a smile to that person's face in a way that will be appreciated.

65

TURNING A STRANGER INTO A FRIEND

When I was a child, I was shy and timid. I remember how often I was impressed with my father's ability to speak to each stranger as a new friend. Whether he was speaking to a store-keeper in a store he had never been in before, whether total strangers asked him for blessings and prayers, or whether he needed to ask someone for directions, everyone was treated as a friend.

Growing up I felt that I would never be able to do the same. Fortunately, I was wrong. When you have a role model for a specific behavior, you might think that this is totally not you. But if you have seen someone doing something positive even once, you have a role model to emulate.

When you view each stranger as a friend, you will always be in the presence of friends. Your facial expression and tone of voice will convey a friendly message and the vast majority of people will reciprocate. As King Solomon in his wisdom said (*Proverbs* 27:19), "Just as with water, the face [in the water] reflects the face [of the observer], so, too, is the heart of one person to another." The Vilna Gaon (1720-1797) explains, "Whatever expression is on your face when you look into water, that is the expression you will see staring back at you. So, too, if you feel positive about another person, that person will feel positive towards you. But if inwardly you feel negative towards someone, even if you do not verbally say anything bad to him, he will have negative feelings towards you" (see *Consulting the Wise,* pp.19-20).

It was over 10 years ago when I was speaking to someone who was about to accept a new position in which he would need to establish rapport with total strangers. He loved teaching but was concerned that some people would come to his lectures, not because they really wanted to, but because sponsors of the program would invite them to come and they would not be able to refuse.

I suggested that once someone shows up to a class he would give, he should view them as cherished friends. He asked me how to do this. While it was the first time I ever tried this, I told him to follow me and watch what I would do. We were in the Aish Hatorah Center in the Old City of Jerusalem. We went outside and waited by the top of the steps that led from the Western Wall towards Jaffa Gate.

After about a minute a middle-aged man who looked like a tourist came along. I entered a consciousness that everyone on the planet was my friend, and greeted this new friend with positive energy.

"Hi there, what city are you from?" I asked him.

"From Baltimore," he replied.

"That's amazing," I said. "I'm from Baltimore also. I grew up on

Fairmount Avenue, near Patterson Park, and my father was the rabbi of a synagogue on Lombard Street."

"I know the neighborhood well," he replied.

We spoke for a few moments about our favorite memories of living in Baltimore. And then I bid him farewell.

He shook my hand with enthusiasm, and said to me, "It was really great to have met you."

My long-time friend came over to me and said, "That person really looked like he became your friend."

"I told you he would," I said. "I'm not always in that state myself. But when I am and utilize it selectively it's powerful."

Go out of your way to treat people who would appreciate it as friends. We all share the same planet, we all need oxygen, we all have a common ancestry, and whatever our differences we still have much that is similar. Besides contributing to the happiness of others, you add much happiness to your own life.

66

SPEAK AS YOU WISH TO BE SPOKEN TO

"I do not know why, but some people I talk to make me feel wonderful and others make me feel awful. What they say does not seem that drastically different. I wonder what the key element is."

Sound is energy. This is a highly significant statement that affects you every time you speak to someone. Your tone of voice creates a specific type of energy. A soft and smooth tone of voice creates peaceful energy. An upbeat or joyous tone of voice creates positive energy. Both of these are in stark contrast to an angry tone of voice that creates an angry loop.

When you speak, your tone of voice creates either positive or distressful feelings in the person on the receiving end of that energy. The other person is likely to speak back to you in a tone that is similar to your own. For this reason King Solomon (*Proverbs* 15:1) advises us: "A soft reply turns away anger." A soft tone of voice has a calming effect both on you — the speaker — and on the listener.

Do you want others to speak to you in an upbeat tone of voice? Then speak to them that way. A word of caution: For some people an overly enthusiastic tone of voice is too intense. Observe the effects of how you speak and modify your intensity according to the reaction of the listener.

If someone speaks to you in a tone of voice that causes you distress, ask that person in a polite, respectful manner, "Please speak in a pleasant tone of voice." Or, "Could you please speak in the same tone of voice that you used when you spoke on the telephone?" If the other person does not change his tone of voice, try whispering and notice its effects. Often, this works well.

A tool for raising your own spirits is to talk enthusiastically on a topic that you are excited about. If you are in a low mood, one way to raise it is to think of a person with whom you can share an idea in an enthusiastic tone of voice and contact that person.

You can even start talking enthusiastically about something you have not been enthusiastic about before. As you speak this way, your state will improve.

When you speak to someone whose tone of voice is serene or joyous, mirror it. As you mirror that tone of voice, you begin to make it your own.

67.
IT IS NOT PERSONAL

"If you do not accept my invitation, I'll be very hurt."

"If you do not eat what I cook or bake, I'll be insulted."

"If you disagree with my opinion, I'll be angry at you."

"If you do not remember…, I'll be depressed."

You have a choice whether or not to take things personally. Those who consider it important to be happy will choose not to take things that others say or do or fail to say and do as personal attacks on them. They realize that each individual has his or her own reasons and motives for doing or not doing things. People do what they do because they feel that is what is best for them. Each person has his or her personal tastes and interests. What others say or do is based on their perceptions of a situation and is not necessarily based on the total reality.

I remember an incident when my married daughter was a young teenager and baked a cake. A younger brother commented, "I do not like this cake."

"That's o.k. with me," she said with equanimity. "It's just a cake I baked and has nothing to do with me as a person."

I was in the room during this conversation and felt proud of this rational response.

I have come across many instances when people have become more religious than their parents. Some parents are understanding if their children's new dietary standards necessitate refraining from eating food that they have eaten previously. But others angrily say, "If you do not eat our food the way you used to, I will take it personally." These parents create misery for everyone concerned. Why choose to take it personally when you do not really have to?

Besides causing oneself unnecessary unhappiness by taking things personally, it is also a move to control and manipulate others. "You must do what I want you to do or else I will get angry at you," and, "If you do not agree with me, I will cause you distress." The threat of anger or disapproval is supposed to influence the receiver of this communication to act in certain ways or to agree with a position that he or she does not really agree with. Many peace-loving people prefer to give in rather than to argue and quarrel. But the dubious winner is really a loser, He is arbitrarily making his self-esteem dependent on the subjective opinions and tastes of another person.

How do you avoid the distress caused by taking things personally? First, realize that your value and worth are a given. Your Creator has given you intrinsic value and nothing anyone else says or does can take this away from you. Integrating this awareness frees you from feeling lessened in any way by other people's words and actions. Other people can lower themselves by being insensitive or inconsiderate to you. But the only person who can really lower your self-esteem is you yourself. When you perceive your true value, it will remain healthy and intact. Your emotional state might be temporarily lowered, but never your value.

Realize the wisdom of the saying, "There is no arguing over matters of taste and smell." People have different tastes, different interests, different priorities, different criteria, and attribute different meanings to the same thing. Therefore if a person makes a choice of words or deeds that is not to your liking, that is their issue, not yours.

In short, appreciate the positive things that people say to you and do for you. And view the negative as either their limitations or their subjective tastes, or as a helpful message for you to improve in some way. This approach makes you an emotional winner.

68

FORGIVE!

"I cannot forgive my parents for not understanding me better."

"I cannot forgive my teachers for not making me work harder."

"I cannot forgive my friend for not inviting me to his party."

"I cannot forgive my husband for not remembering my birthday."

"I cannot forgive my employer for not choosing me for the vacated position."

"I cannot forgive anyone who ever insulted me."

When these people do not forgive others, who are they harming? Themselves most of all, and at times, only themselves. If you do not forgive, that means that you will be feeling resentment and anger. And these are mutually exclusive with happiness.

Consistently happy people are either in one of two conditions; Either no one has ever wronged or slighted them in any way, or else they have forgiven those who have. Since it is almost impossible not to have been wronged or slighted, if you want to master happiness, you need to learn how to forgive.

Forgiving is like floating on water. You do not need to do anything. You just need to let go. When you were a young child of 5 or 6, you became angry at your brothers, sisters, friends, and classmates. You might have even said, "I will not forgive you." Now when you look back at the vast majority of those situations, you will see that they were trivial. It is presently easy for you to forgive someone for not giving you a bite of their ice cream, not letting you play with their toys, or grabbing your ice cream or toys. Just as you have already forgiven them, you will be able to forgive others for more recent events when you realize that most things are trivial when compared to your emotional and spiritual well-being.

We all need our Creator's forgiveness. By forgiving others we elevate ourselves and render ourselves more worthy of being forgiven. When you find it difficult to forgive, pray with your own words for the strength to forgive.

A wise observer of human nature pointed out, "People who don't forgive usually do so for a personal benefit." It often gives a nonforgiver a sense of power. It meets one's needs for revenge. It can be manipulatively used to get concessions from someone.

At times the pain is still too strong to let go. That is understandable. But never go out of your way to hold onto resentment. The benefits are not worth the cost of what it does to your physical, emotional, and spiritual health.

It can take time to forgive if someone wronged you in a serious way. But when a matter is not major, forgive. A level to strive for is to forgive a person who sincerely regrets his wrong. But this will still leave you open to resentment towards those who do not realize the pain they caused or do not have the strength of character to ask for forgiveness. So a wise person will forgive others even if they do not ask for forgiveness. If you value your happiness, you will make this your custom. Some do this nightly before they go to sleep. Others wait. But do not wait too long. Your happiness is too precious.

"When I forgave my parents for not treating me the way a child should be treated, I began a new relationship with them. Now I have a father and mother. What a shame that I did not realize the power of forgiveness before."

"I forgave my employer. Our relationship improved and he went out of his way to help me in ways that he would not have if I would have held onto my resentment."

"I forgave my husband for not remembering my birthday. Having loving harmony in our home is much more valuable than a gift."

"I still do not like insults, but holding on to them makes me suffer from them over and over again. I now realize that it's wiser to transcend them and let them go."

69.
COMPASSION FOR THE UNKIND

hose who radiate unconditional love and sincere kindness are happy people. Their essential goodness is an integral part of their positive emotional states. On the other side of the scale, we all have encountered people who are mean, short tempered, spiteful, grudge bearing, vengeful, violent, or hateful. Some have small traces of these attributes. For others, this is their essence. There is a common denominator to all of them. They are unhappy.

It is easy to be intimidated by mean people. See through their mask. Underneath is an insecure and unhappy person. They are alienated from others because they are alienated from themselves. Have compassion for them — not pity, not condemning, not fear, but compassion. Feel for their suffering. Identify with their core humanity. You might be able to influence them for the good. You might not. Either way your compassion frees you from their destructiveness. And if you would like to help them change, compassion gives you a chance to succeed.

You cannot feign compassion. You can act kind. You can act polite. You can act with respect. You can even speak as if you were empathetic. But compassion is a quality that needs to actually be experienced to be considered compassion. Compassion necessitates a basic respect for the person for whom you feel compassion. You identify with that person. You see that person's potential. Being a recipient of true compassion is healing. True compassion builds self-esteem. True compassion is the ultimate in acts of kindness.

What if you would like to be compassionate, but do not actually experience it? Then be understanding. Understanding is intellectual. It is valuable in itself, and is an important step towards becoming compassionate. When you understand someone and see his total life history and situation, it is easier to be kind. This helps the recipient of your kindness and elevates you spiritually and emotionally.

Pray in your own words for compassion. A compassionate person is a spiritual person. A mean person lacks a connection with the Source of all Compassion. Your compassion is your emulating our Creator. There is an emotional price for compassion. With compassion you feel the pain of others. But this elevates you and gives you a perspective that will permeate your entire life with an elevating spirituality.

I grew up with gentle parents. They were consistently kind and caring. I was not mentally prepared to cope well with tough, rough, or mean people. They seemed so much stronger and more confident than I was. When it was pointed out to me that unkind people are invariably unhappy, it gave me more confidence to cope with them. I no longer looked at them as all powerful. Rather, I saw the scared little child hidden within. I was dedicated not to give over my own inner empowerment to anyone who did not treat others with the basic respect due to every human being. My own inner confidence enabled me to speak up in a way that brought out the respect of such people and they began to treat me better. This was a reaction that I would not have believed before I actually experienced it.

70

TRANSCENDING INSULTS

The power of anyone else to cause you distress with an insult is the power you give that person. Do not empower anyone to cause you pain. You are too valuable and precious to relinquish your power to someone who is committing the crime of trying to verbally harm another human being, which happens to be you.

Words are harmless in themselves even though they can be powerful. It is you, the receiver of those words, who is the ultimate decider of whether or not someone's insensitive words will be distressful.

What are the thoughts and attitudes that enable someone else's words to cause you pain? "It's awful if someone talks to me like this." "These words are so powerful that I am powerless to stop them from hurting me." "I used to suffer if anyone spoke to me this way in the past. I must suffer again now." "It's my very nature to be hurt if someone talks to me this way." "I must be an inferior person if someone says this to me." "It always takes me days to overcome an insult."

When suffering from insults, the reaction is so swift and automatic that many people consider themselves helpless to prevent their suffering. But it is your personal interpretation of what is said that creates your reaction. Regardless of how you have reacted in the past, right now you can create new reactions. The ultimate reaction is to enjoy transcending insults.

Develop a spiritual awareness that if the Almighty is sending you an experience it is for your growth and development. If someone says something insulting to you, learn from it to be more careful not to cause anyone else pain with words. Learn from it to spread the consciousness that it is wrong to use one's power of speech to cause suffering to others.

Words are energy in the form of sound waves that this person is directing towards you. Say to yourself, "This energy will empower me." Feel the energy empowering you as you keep repeating this. Not everyone can do this right away. If you do not yet find this working for you, be patient and try again a different time.

Learn from your own reactions to find your vulnerable spots. You are valuable. Be committed to increase your feelings of self-worth and self-esteem to such a degree that no one else can decrease them. View a negative reaction to an insult as a reminder to increase and enhance your awareness of your immense value. The Creator and Sustainer of the universe has given it to you. No mortal can ever take it away.

Hear an inner voice telling you, "You are valuable. This person's put-down is his problem and demeans him. It has everything to do with his faults and nothing to do with your essence as a person."

If someone says something insulting, you can mentally create humorous scenery, pictures, and music that will make you smile.

You can imagine the insulter as a clown, an infant, or as a ridiculously angry idiot. You can imagine the person as a distant mountain or as having a squeaky, high-pitched voice. You can imagine yourself as a powerful giant and this midget's words bounce right off you. You can imagine yourself surrounded by a transparent shield that nothing can penetrate. Mentally practice: Imagine someone insulting you and imagine yourself reacting the way you wish to react. When you repeat this enough times, this will become your reality.

I never thought that I would be able to say this, but I can: Insults no longer bother me. I have made them into a humorous game. I used to be supersensitive. I would feel tremendously hurt by even minor insults. Now I can easily handle any insult thrown my way. I realized that I have the power to tell myself, "The more anyone insults me, the greater joy I will create for myself." I imagine a crowd of a million fans cheering for me. This drowns out the insult and I bask in the glow of the wonderful feelings I create through my imagery.

71.
AVOID THE NEGATIVITY VIRUS

We human beings were created to be influenced by others. Our goal is to utilize this natural tendency to emulate and learn from positive role models. When you are in the presence of people with elevated character traits, you yourself become a better person.

Because of our tendency to take on the attitudes, perspectives, reframes, and emotional states of others, we should spend as much time as possible in the presence of those who enable us to create positive outlooks and states. And we need to avoid the negativity of others. And when this is not possible, at least to minimize its effects.

Some people tend to see what is wrong with each situation. They keep predicting disasters and catastrophes even though they have been wrong many times. "Isn't this awful," is one of their favorite sentences. These same people tend to see faults in others. They will judge them negatively, even though it would be relatively easy to judge them favorably. Be careful not to catch their negativity virus. It can be contagious.

Be aware of how various people affect your thinking and your emotional states. You might have been quite happy in a given situation, but a negative person might view it in a totally different light and can drag you down. You might have viewed a person you interact with positively and rightly so. But a negative person points out minor faults and disregards all of his positive qualities. The next time you see this person you might see him differently than before. He is the same person, but you are not. You have been contaminated with negativity. Make an effort to once again identify the person with his positive attributes and have the courage to ask the spreader of negativity to stop. "I want to hear other people saying positive things about you, and I would like you to do the same about others."

When you hear negative statements from others, counter them with positive reframes. When possible, speak up and tell the other person your positive perspective. When you cannot speak up, counteract the negativity in your own mind. The more negative someone speaks, the more positive you can be. Let their negativity be a trigger for your positivity.

72

ASK FOR WHAT YOU WANT

A question I am frequently asked is, "You emphasize the importance of appreciating what one has, but will not that prevent me from trying to improve my present situation?"

The Sages (*Ethics of the Fathers* 4:1) define a wealthy person as one who takes pleasure in what he has. They advised us to experience joy, but did not state that we should refrain from trying to improve our situation. There are two diverse patterns to choose from when a situation is not to our liking.

One pattern is as follows: "It is awful that things are not the way I want them to be. I hate it when I am not getting what I wish for. I will keep complaining about this and maybe my complaining will get me what I want." The owner of this pattern suffers, and is not traveling along the path that will lead to a desired destination. He complains, but does so in a counterproductive manner.

A more effective pattern is the following: "Things are not the way I want them to be. If I am not able to change the situation, I will accept it and focus on what is going right in my life. But I will see if I can communicate in a way that will influence and persuade others to help me get the outcome that I wish for."

The owner of this pattern gains in two ways. First of all, there is a possibility that a way will be found to achieve the desired outcome. Second, if the outcome is not achieved, there is at least a willingness to accept reality and to make the best of the situation.

In my counseling experience I have witnessed many instances of people failing to communicate with an outcome in mind. If I am able to teach outcome thinking to an individual or a couple, their lives are changed. Not focusing on your desired outcome is like saying, "I really want to go somewhere but I will not do anything to ensure that I will be going on the right road to get there. And if the road I happen to take does not get me to the destination I was hoping for, I will sit by the side of the road and cry. I will blame others, but I certainly will not look for a map that might show me the best way to get where I hope to go." Don't you just feel like calling out to this person, "Get a map. And if you do not know how to get a map yourself, ask someone who knows the way for directions."

How can you master the pattern of outcome thinking? The way you master any skill is through practice. So practice using the desired pattern over and over again until it becomes second nature.

Keep asking yourself, "What is the outcome that I would like?" Then choose what seems to you the best way to get that outcome. If one approach does not work, try another one. At times you might not be able to think of a workable approach. But if you do not think about what you wish to say with a specific outcome in mind, you are almost certainly assuring yourself of failure. And it is obvious that this is not anyone's outcome of choice.

73

COPING WITH DIFFICULTIES

"Has not your life been difficult?" I asked this joyous elderly man who smiled easily and had great energy even for someone much younger than him.

"It sure has, and I am grateful for every minute. An easy job is boring. I love challenges. I grew up in a home without much money, and my own businesses have had many ups and downs. I enjoy the ups and do not let the downs keep me down for very long. I am not perfect, but I enjoy improving. I have had a number of operations in the last few years, but as soon as I feel better, I put them behind me."

It seems to me that a key to this man's general level of happiness was his awareness that life is not always easy, but it can be enjoyable. You will be faced with difficulties regardless of your attitude towards them. By developing a positive attitude towards them, your life will be much more enjoyable.

Be aware of the inner resources that will help you cope better with the difficulties you face. It could be courage, creativity, humor, acceptance, patience, spiritual awareness, persistence, and tenacity. Each difficulty you face develops your character. Every difficulty teaches you something. Coping well with one difficulty can make it easier for you to cope better with future challenging situations.

Visualize yourself coping with difficulties the way you would wish. Also, learn from role models who are able to handle similar difficulties the way you would like to. Ask them for the beliefs and attitudes that enable them to cope as well as they do.

When you face a difficulty, pray in your own words for Divine assistance. Your difficulty then becomes a vehicle that will elevate you and intensify your connection with G-d.

When you master the ability to enjoy difficulties, you will view them as challenges and tests and you will find them becoming easier to handle.

74

THE IMPERFECTION OF PERFECTIONISM

"I kept doing well. But I was not perfect so I felt like a failure."

"I was always told, 'You can do better,' as a child. So I find it difficult to be satisfied with anything I do since I know I really could do better."

"If I make a slight mistake, I focus on it and take what I did right for granted."

Perfectionism and happiness do not go hand in hand. The human condition is imperfection. And that is why there is always more work to do in this world. And that is what will enable us to maintain humility even if we did accomplish a lot. But we need to maintain a sense of joy even though we are not perfect. We were never meant to be perfect. But it is our mission to learn and to improve.

Perfectionism is the attitude, "It's either 100 percent or it's a total failure." In some areas this could be true. A serious operation that was almost successful failed if the patient died. If an airplane pilot almost made a safe landing but the plane crashed, it was a total failure for all those who were killed in the crash. But in the vast majority of the things we do, perfection might be nice, but it would not make too much of a difference.

A perfectionist is nervous the entire time. "What if it's not perfect?" they repeat to themselves. There are many ways that this would not be perfect and only one that would be considered perfect. Enjoy the positive activities that you are engaged in. Enjoy every bit of success. And enjoy the entire process of improving.

I found it ironic that when I gave up my quest for perfection, I worked faster than before. I enjoyed what I was doing and felt calmer. This enabled me to think clearer and sharpened my skills. I was always afraid that if I would not try to be perfect, I would do an inferior job. Now I see that my basic intentions were right. But my approach was wrong. Instead of being nervous all the time, I am now excited about watching my progress.

75

YOURSELF: THE ONLY ONE WHO CAN REJECT YOU

Feeling rejected can be highly painful. When someone feels rejected, it is often not only the present loss that hurts, but his self-image is challenged. People differ in how long it takes them to overcome rejection. And the range can vary greatly, for some people recover fairly rapidly while others suffer intensely for a long period of time.

But nobody can actually reject you. They can say that they are not interested in purchasing something that you are selling or using your services. They can say that they are not interested in publishing something that you have written. They can say that they are not interested in marrying you. They can even say that they are not interested in meeting you. But no one can actually reject "you." No other person can really know everything about you and who you are. What some people label rejection is really another person not yet deciding to buy what you are selling, to hire your services, to publish your article or book, to marry you, or to meet you. At times you might be able to convince someone who originally said, "No" to say, "Yes." And the more positive your state and your feelings about yourself, the greater chance of your accomplishing this.

Realize that if you choose not to reject yourself, others can choose to say, "No," but you yourself do not need to feel rejected. You can never be certain that this "No" is not the best thing that could have happened, as later events might show. Since it is impossible to know all the consequences of this "No," choose to delay judgment on whether or not, in the long term, this was not the best thing that could have happened. Do not choose to feel needless pain about something that might actually turn out quite well.

Feeling rejected is a sign that one's brain is still in need of an upgrading and this can be valuable information. It certainly can increase one's humility which is a valuable attribute to increase. And the more upgraded the brain, the more it will appreciate the benefits of humility and therefore will cherish every opportunity to gain more of it.

If you ever do feel distress because of feeling rejected, use this as a learning experience to have more compassion for others who suffer. If the "rejecter" insensitively chose words that were more painful than necessary, learn more tactful ways to say, "No." You might ask other people, "Have you ever experienced someone saying, 'No,' to you so tactfully that you did not feel bad?" Answers to this question can be passed along to others and therefore one's own suffering will be the root cause of saving other people from similar distress. An upgraded brain will appreciate this.

I interviewed a very successful fundraiser. "You always seem pretty joyous. I'm certain that many people refuse to give you money. How do you cope with the rejection?" I asked him.

"Nobody has ever rejected me," he replied.

"But surely not everyone you ask for a donation gives it to you."

"That's right," he said. "But if they do not give me a donation it's only because they are either not financially able to do so at the time, or else they do not realize the great value of giving this donation. The organization I collect for is truly worthwhile. Perhaps I did not approach this person in the right way. If that's the case, asking the right way is a skill that I keep getting better at. This is a statement about my present ability to influence and persuade which I keep upgrading. Those who take a refusal as a personal statement about their value and worth are making a serious mistake. One's value and worth is a given and is never on the line."

76.
PREPARING FOR ADVERSITY

"I do not want to even think of the possibility of things going wrong."

"When the unexpected happens, I easily become overwhelmed."

"My mother would fall apart when faced with difficulties. I'm afraid that I inherited her 'fall-apart genes.'"

The best time to mentally prepare yourself for times of adversity is when things are going well and you are in a resourceful state. Adversity is a challenge that enables you to develop attributes that would not be developed in easier times. Keep building up the inner resources that will enable you to cope well with difficulties. If you are in the middle of a difficulty right now, then right now is the best time to build up those resources. You will not have to wait and see if the inner resources you need are becoming a part of you; you will see results right away.

Develop courage and confidence. Develop persistence and resilience. Develop optimism and hope. How can you develop these qualities? Visualize yourself mastering them. See, hear, and feel yourself being confident and courageous. See, hear, and feel yourself persisting and bouncing back. Right now feel an inner sense of optimism that you will cope well with difficulties. And if a difficulty arises that you do not cope with as well as you wished, learn from the experience to cope better next time.

Every time you hear a story about someone who handled difficulties and challenges gracefully and with inner strength learn from it. Picture yourself being able to handle similar situations as well as that person.

One of the most amazing stories of courage and transcendence is the description of the murder of Rabbi Akiva. The Talmud relates how Rabbi Akiva, who died a painful martyr's death, remained calm and peaceful during his final moments. He totally transcended the torture of the Romans and serenely recited his final *Shema Yisrael,* his affirmation of faith in the Creator.

"Our teacher, how can you remain so serene at a time like this?" his students called out to him.

They wanted to learn one last lesson from him before he departed from this world.

"My entire life I prepared myself for this moment," he said with his waning energy. That is, he consistently pictured himself dying serenely with the declaration of the *Shema* on his lips.

Rabbi Akiva taught us all to attach ourselves to our Creator and with this inspiration and elevation we will be able to cope with adversity. This visualization prepares us for greatness and is a great act in itself.

77.
GROWING FROM GUILT

When we experience guilt, it is because we realize that we have not lived up to the standards and values that we know or feel we should. Guilt can be very appropriate at times. Yes, we really made a mess of things. Yes, we really shouted at someone or said things that we know we should not have said. We have caused others pain. We might have done things for which we presently are embarrassed. They might have been major or even relatively minor, but we should have known better or acted wiser. And now we feel guilty because we should have had greater self-mastery even if we were under pressure and stress. We might be feeling guilty because of something we did not do or say, and now it is self-evident to us what we should have done or said.

Use guilt to upgrade your present consciousness and way of being. Guilt means that you have a more elevated awareness now than before. See yourself reliving the past in a way that your higher values would have wanted you to live them. See yourself living a better life in the future because of the underlying values that created that guilt and now creates a better you.

Guilt is negative if someone just wallows in these distressful feelings and fails to take action to make amends. Guilt is negative if a person feels so discouraged because of those feelings that he does not engage in positive behavior and actions in the present. Guilt is positive if it prevents you from harming others. Guilt is positive if it motivates you to live life on a higher level. Guilt is positive if it leads to improvement and an upgrading of your character.

A person who never regrets his wrongdoings is likely to repeat them. But excessive guilt is harmful. An important factor concerning regret is whether a person feels bad that he feels bad, or feels good about his regret. With negative guilt feelings, a person feels bad about feeling bad. With positive regret, a person appreciates his feeling bad about doing something improper because it manifests a sense of decent values and ideals on his part.

Ask yourself, "Will my blaming myself help me improve or not?" To the degree self-blame motivates you to change for the better, it is positive. Self-blame that prevents improvement is counterproductive and should be overcome. When you stop feeling self-pity over your mistakes, your mind will be free to work on improvement. And when your brain focuses on self-improvement, it is in the process of upgrading itself.

If you experience guilt, stop and ask yourself, "What can I do to make amends for the wrong that I have done?" It might be going out of your way to be kind and giving to someone you have harmed. It might be a comprehensive increase of compassion and generosity. It might be elevating your general behavior. When your guilt leads to upgraded behavior, you have grown from the experience even though you wish you would have gained the same growth and development in more positive ways. We cannot turn the clock back but we can upgrade ourselves right now. That is the wisest choice.

I was ruining my life, but kept denying it. The way I was treating others caused them much distress, but I felt everyone else deserved it. They irritated me and were the cause of my anger. I kept alienating people without realizing to what extent. Then a good friend of mine had the courage to give me a heart-to-heart talk. He asked me not to interrupt him and I gave him my word that I would let him speak uninterrupted. He spoke to me for over an hour and I was devastated. I am forever grateful to him for ending our talk by saying, 'I realize that what I told you was painful. I hope that it will be painful enough for you to change the way you treat other people. I will gladly give you feedback if you want. But it's up to you.' I never felt so awful and miserable my entire life. But that day was a day of transformation for me. It was over 10 years ago, and I consider it one of the greatest days of my life. Those who meet me for the first time now would never believe the distance I traveled.

78

DO NOT WHINE UNLESS YOU ENJOY IT

The full title of this formula is: "Do not whine unless you enjoy it. And if you enjoy it, know that there are better things to enjoy."

Whiners and kvetches do so for various reasons. Deep down they enjoy it. They like to complain and blame. They like the attention and sympathy this gives them. Their favorite topic is what is wrong in their lives. They find whining to be their most enjoyable choice of what to talk about.

Another reason people whine is because they have formed this habit. They do get more pleasure talking about and doing other things, but they somehow forget to do so.

We all need empathy at times. When we are in a crisis or are feeling overwhelmed, an empathetic listening ear can be a life-saver. When you need to share your pain with someone, this is not whining. This is a valid emotional need and others should validate your feelings, just as you should validate the feelings of others. When you are in emotional pain, talking about the causes can give you a sense of perspective. The very act of speaking to someone with a sympathetic ear lightens the burden.

Whining that is problematic comes into play when you overdo it. The need for empathy differs. Individuals with more intense emotions and more difficult life situations need more empathy than people who have less emotional natures and easier life situations.

As soon as you hear yourself whining, ask yourself, "What would be better for me to do now?"

Find solutions instead of whining. If you cannot find a total solution, a partial solution is better than none. "What can I do to improve the situation?" is a great question.

If you whine over something that happened in the past, realize that you still have a choice. Since you cannot change that past, you choose how long you want to focus on the distressful thoughts of something that is unchangeable. Unhappy people choose to spend a lot of time on this. Happy people choose thoughts and actions that make their life better.

I used to be a whiner. My mother was one and so was her mother. You could even call it a family tradition. If my husband or anyone else would suggest that I develop a more positive pattern, I would angrily say, "You're so insensitive."

My husband would defend himself by telling me that if something really bothered me, he was totally open to hear me out as long as it would take for me to overcome my pain. He would do anything he could to lessen my distress. "But you are causing yourself unnecessary pain by talking all the time about all the things you do not like," he would say. But I just respond-

ed by telling him, "You do not understand what it is like."

The turning point for me was the week I stayed in a hospital for minor surgery. I had a roommate who was the biggest kvetch I ever met. Everyone in the hospital is in pain. Expressing the pain lessens it. But I saw the difference between those who were able to transcend the pain and those on the other extreme who wallowed in it. This I could accept. But my roommate complained about everything possible. At first I had hope that she would finally run out of things to complain about. But I soon saw that she did not and would not. She complained about everything that ever went wrong in her life. She did not have any limiting rules when it came to complaining. She would complain about the same things over and over again. Not only was every day another day to repeat the same complaints, but in the same day she would complain about things she had already complained about that day.

I hated to listen to her incessant complaining. "Is this how awful I sound when I complain?" I asked myself. And the answer was obvious. I resolved to change the way I spoke. When I had a real problem or difficulty I would discuss it. But I would no longer complain just out of habit. I was resolved to speak about more pleasant topics. I felt great joy when my husband told me, "You are so much more pleasant to listen to since you came home from the hospital." I knew it was not the hospital, but my roommate who was a messenger to enlighten me.

79.
GAINING FROM SETBACKS

"What motivated you to start your own business?" I asked the wealthy owner of a major company.

"I was fired from my job, and decided that I wanted to be my own boss," was his reply.

"The two of you have been happily married for over 30 years. How did you meet?"

"I was engaged to someone whom I had known for a long time. We got into many silly arguments. I felt devastated, however, when a week before the wedding I received a telephone call that the wedding was off. A few months later, I met my life partner who is everything I wished for."

"I am now a lecturer in a major educational institution. I have accomplished more than I had ever dreamed when I was a teenager. I look back at how the institution of higher learning that I wanted to attend did not accept me as a student. While I felt awful that day, it was the best thing that ever happened to me. I wish that I would have realized how it would eventually turn out at the time I felt rejected."

"How did you become an expert on this topic?" I asked this successful lecturer.

"I did not do very well in school. The day the principal called me into his office and told me that I could not graduate with the other students in my class was my turning point. I decided that I needed to find one area which I would focus on and this has become my life's mission. Today, I am consulted about my areas of expertise by large companies and I lecture in many different cities."

Setbacks are a natural part of living. Grow from each one. You have learned something. At times the setback itself can even be the start of something that will be wonderful for you. At all times you can make a wise choice to begin again with renewed energy and vigor.

"How can I benefit from this?" This one question will transform your losses into gains. It is the proverbial making lemonade out of a lemon. As you think of potential benefits, it saves you from counterproductive thinking and points you in the right direction.

Be creative when you seek benefits. A creative benefit might not be obvious at first. But once you find it, your view of what happened will go from negative to positive. Also, be patient. We all have gained from what at first seemed to be a setback, but eventually proved to be a major step forward in our lives. Your next apparent setback could be the greatest thing that ever happened to you.

80

DEFEAT: A STEPPING STONE FOR GROWTH

In everyone's life there are moments of defeat. No one is always victorious. In victory you gain from celebration. In defeat you gain from the potential for nobility of spirit, from greater humility, from increased compassion and understanding for others who also suffer, from gaining a deeper and more profound way of being, from connecting with the Creator in a way that only the submissiveness of defeat will enable you to do.

"Everything in life serves as a challenge and test to elevate us" (*Path of the Just,* Ch.1). For those who develop a comprehensive spiritual awareness there is not a major difference between victory and defeat. Both are potentially elevating tests. It is not the external event that counts. Rather, it is your growing from this event. Defeat is your opportunity to speak and act in ways that express your awareness that the purpose of life is to connect with the Creator in this world and for all eternity. Although the defeat will have an effect on your present emotional state, ultimately your spirit will be raised.

One's self-esteem can easily be battered by defeat. Your value as a person is given to you at birth. You are created in the Creator's image and you are His child. Whether you win or lose, your intrinsic value and immense worth stay constant. Integrating this awareness gives your self-esteem a greater sense of stability.

Part of the difficulty of defeat is the shock effect. The more a person thinks that victory is a certainty, the more pain is caused by defeat. Knowing that victory and defeat are in the hand of our Creator, one knows that victory is never a certainty. The person whose main value is his own ego can be shattered by defeat. The person whose main value is connecting with the Creator will consider defeat another tool and exercise to attain that glorious goal.

I ran for school president. All of my friends told me that I was sure to win. I was bright and popular. I got excellent grades and had many great friends. I remember the shock and pain I felt when it was announced that my opponent won. "How could this have happened?" I asked myself.

I asked some students who I thought would give me an objective answer. Some voted for the other person because they wanted to help an underdog. They felt they would be doing an act of kindness by helping someone whose self-esteem needed a boost. A minority of students voted against me because they were envious of me. And some felt that they needed to teach me a lesson not to be so conceited.

The latter were successful. It would be conceited for me to think that I lost all of my arrogance. But I can honestly say that this defeat was a positive turning point in my life. Since then I have decreased my self-centeredness and increased my focus on our Heavenly Father and His other children.

Looking back at this event of 40 years ago, I see that what I considered a defeat was a step towards many true victories in spirituality and interpersonal relationships.

81.
THINKING ABOUT PROBLEMS

"Are you saying that we should never think of problems?"

"Do you meant to tell me not to talk about what bothers and distresses me?"

"Are you advocating blinding myself from reality?"

"Are you against planning to deal with potential misfortunes?"

The answer to all these questions is one word — a loud and clear "NO!"

A wise person differentiates between productive and counterproductive thinking and speaking. We need to think about problems to solve them. At times the only way to overcome sad and painful feelings is to discuss them with those who can help alleviate them. Knowing that we are heard and understood can lighten our burden. We need to keep our eyes open to reality and the wise person sees what will be and intelligently formulates the best possible plan.

Unhappy people think of problems without spending enough time working on solutions. Unhappy people spend way too much time on what bothers and distresses them and not enough time on what they appreciate and enjoy. The reality of people who make themselves needlessly unhappy is distorted. They make arbitrary and subjectively negative reframes and mistakenly think that it is objective reality. For some reason they think their negative way of looking at things is more real than sensible and intelligent positive ways. Unhappy people do not plan to make things better. They tend to obsessively dwell on exactly what they do not like. Because they do not want to be unhappy, they paradoxically keep focusing exactly on what makes them unhappy, which is not the most advisable course of action.

We are recommending and advocating spending most of your mental focus on what you appreciate and enjoy. We are recommending and advocating the mastery of sensible and intelligent positive reframes. We are recommending and advocating taking positive action to prevent and solve problems. And we are recommending and advocating the development of a joyous way of being. When you are in positive, resourceful states, you think clearer about problems and difficulties and you are more likely to come up with workable and effective solutions.

82

"AND THEN WHAT?"

"I do not want to ask because the answer might be, 'No.' "

"I'm afraid I'll be screamed at."

"People might stare at me."

"Someone might laugh."

Did you ever refrain from doing something you felt you should or could do because you feared being: (a) told "no"; (b) screamed at; (c) stared at; (d) laughed at? The amazing thing about these common fears is that they are totally groundless.

If someone says, "No," at least you had the courage to ask. By not asking, you certainly will not get what you wanted. By asking, you had a chance.

If someone screams at you, stares at you, or laughs at you, you will not melt. The only power someone's screaming, staring, or laughing at you has over you is the power you let it have. Your brain can focus on something else that you enjoy thinking about. And when you do, these reactions of others will be rendered harmless. You might even find a creative reframe to make the encounter easier to handle or even profitable or enjoyable. For example, if someone were to offer you a large amount of money if someone would scream, stare, or laugh, you would be joyous. Now you can imagine that happening and enjoy your mental imagery. This is much more sensible than allowing someone's insensitivity to cause you more pain than necessary.

You can also view each such incident as another step towards gaining immunity from the fear of other people's reactions. When you see that you are able to handle any of these incidents better than you thought, you will be on your way to gain freedom from worrying about them.

One question that is effective in rendering these types of situations harmless is: "And then what will happen?"

- *If someone says, "No," then what will happen?*
- *If someone screams at you, then what will happen?*
- *If someone stares, then what will happen?*
- *If someone laughs at something you said or did, then what will happen?*

The only negative thing will usually be that the recipient of a "no," a scream, a stare, or a laugh will feel bad. It will not cost you any money, nor will you be physically harmed. And the greater control you have over your brain, the less distress you will feel.

You can build up your inner courage and feel good about yourself. You can build up humility and feel your character developing.

You can think of something that is funny about this or something else and laugh.

So keep asking yourself, "And then what will happen?" If the answer is, "Nothing," it is a shame to allow "nothing" to prevent you from positive action and behavior out of illusory fear. And when you overcome these fears, what will happen is that you will experience more pleasant feelings and less distressful ones.

83

DO NOT ADD TO UNPLEASANTNESS

"I was having a great time that day, until someone gave me a hassle and that ruined the entire day for me."

"That was one of the most enjoyable weddings I ever attended, until someone accidentally spilled wine on me at the end and that ruined the whole wedding for me."

"The vacation was wonderful, but it rained on the last day and I could not do all that I wanted to do. As I look back at that vacation, the main thing that sticks out for me is that feeling of disappointment."

If you were enjoying your day, a wedding, a vacation, or any other experience and something unpleasant happened, allow what you enjoyed to fill your mind. Some people allow minor and trivial distressful things to ruin their day, vacations, and special occasions. In such situations if someone says, "That ruined the whole experience for me," it is their own mental focus that is causing the ruining. What was positive was positive wasn't it? Therefore enjoy what you enjoyed and keep the unpleasantness contained to just the actual time of what you did not enjoy.

I once met a person who did the opposite of allowing small

things to ruin the positive. He would say things like, "Today was a wonderful day. I had a few really exciting moments." "I remember that vacation. The day that sticks out was when I met some new people and had an amazing conversation." "When I was in the hospital, what I liked best was my being able to help alleviate the suffering of the person in the next bed." "I remember that meal. The bread was the type of bread on which you really wanted to make a blessing."

If someone goes on a vacation or attends a banquet, when thinking and talking about it certain parts will be at the forefront of one's mind and other parts will be considered the background. It makes sense to keep the parts you did like at the forefront and the parts you did not like in the background. You do not necessarily want to forget about them. But it is ridiculously stupid to keep allowing minor and trivial annoyances to ruin one's life. How you think about vacations and banquets can easily become the pattern you follow when you think in terms of your entire life. Let the parts you enjoyed be large and colorful in your mind.

If you did not like something that someone said to you, do not keep repeating that part of the conversation. Repeat what you did like. If you did not like something you saw, keep replaying the imagery that you did like, not what you did not. Someone who has a choice of listening to a tape or watching a video will choose the enjoyable. Not many people will say, "I do not like that one, so that is what I will listen to or watch." A tape or video lasts for a short time. Your brain's pattern of focusing on the positive or negative repeats itself again and again and again. So make it a high priority for your brain to see and hear the stuff that enhances your life.

84.
IGNORING THE UNIMPORTANT

Fulfilling your life's mission with joy is what is important. Many other things in life are irrelevant and unimportant. Spend your time on what is truly valuable. And learn to ignore the irrelevant and unimportant.

Those who allow irrelevant and unimportant issues and irritants to dominate their consciousness fail to make the most of their life. They limit themselves spiritually and emotionally. By focusing on the truly valuable and important, you can create a wonderful life for yourself.

A lecture tour brought me to a city not known for its spirituality. I stayed at the home of a colleague. He had a neighbor with whom he had not yet interacted. I started speaking with him and observed that he had a serene nature and positive outlook on life.

"How did you develop such a serene and happy way of being?" I asked him.

"I almost died twice and that taught me to ignore the irrelevant and unimportant," he said to me.

"I had problems with my heart. Just surviving the surgery gave me a greater appreciation for being alive. But what totally transformed me was riding my motorcycle off a cliff. The last thing I saw was the ground rushing to greet me. Then two days later I found myself in a hospital bed in serious condition. I had broken bones and was not certain I would make it. I survived and healed. And now I feel great whenever I wake up in the morning. When I go to sleep, either I will wake up for another day or I will go to a better world. Either way I am a winner."

Our focus is limited. You can choose to focus on what will give you a great life or what will cause frustration, irritation, and unhappiness. By learning to ignore what is unimportant, your brain is free to focus on what is important.

"But how can I ignore things?" many ask. "You do it all the time," I reply. "Every time you walk down a street, you focus on only a limited amount of things. There are buildings, people, cars passing by, the sky, the ground, and so forth. You always pay attention to some things and ignore others. Happy people know what is worthwhile to focus on. Unhappy people forget. Learn to forget to focus on the trivial and irrelevant. And the happier and more joyous you are, the easier this will become."

85.
YOU ARE NOT ALONE

"I worry a lot. It makes me feel alone since most other people do not worry as much as I do."

"I am ashamed to tell anyone how inferior I feel."

"I have a medical condition that limits me. Hardly anyone knows about it. I feel embarrassed to tell others and I feel very alone."

"I do not appreciate what I have. I write lists of what I can appreciate. But it does not work for me. Most other people would appreciate what they have more than I do."

"My anxiety makes me feel that I am alone."

"I felt so relieved when I found out that I'm not the only one who does not experience as much happiness as I imagined everyone else did."

If you are not as happy as you feel you should and could be, know that you are not alone. If you find that nothing seems to work for you, know that you are not alone. If you find that worry, envy, or disappointment blocks your happiness, know that you are not alone. Whatever problems bother you, know that you are not alone.

"Knowing that many others suffer the way you do, is half a consolation." If you lack the happiness you wish for, it is easy to think that you are the only one who feels the way you do. This adds to one's suffering and misery. Each person is unique. But whatever you experience, you can be certain that many others feel the way you do. Most people do not share their inner feelings. You see someone who appears to be happy, but inwardly that person might not be as happy as you think. Some people appear more successful than they actually feel.

The ultimate consolation is the Talmudic concept that the Almighty suffers with His children. When humans suffer, our Creator suffers also, so your suffering is never alone.

In the first chapter of his classic work, *Path of the Just*, Rabbi Moshe Chaim Luzzatto writes that the world we live in is a world of suffering. This, he writes, teaches us that our goal is the eternal existence of our everlasting soul. Knowing that suffering is the norm rather than the exception makes it easier to cope with.

In a one-on-one dialogue, I am often able to point out to people that their experiences are fairly common. Even if the exact details are relatively rare, the general experience of lacking happiness occurs to almost everyone. Still, it is very helpful to find individuals who have experienced the same things you have. Find out from them how they coped. You might find someone you can talk to in person. You might find a book that someone with similar experiences as yours has written. And you might be able to find an empathic and compassionate person who can enter your world and understand your experiences the way you personally experienced them.

Be empathic and compassionate for others who suffer in ways you have not. That person will no longer feel alone, nor will you.

86

FINDING RESOURCE PEOPLE

E very person on our planet is a potential resource for every other person. You are a potential resource for others just as they are for you. So if you cannot find happiness on your own, ask other people to help you.

Other people can be sources of knowledge and inspiration. They can give you tips that you would not have thought of on your own. Do not limit your resources to a relatively small list. A simple example: In most cities if you are lost, the majority of people will try to help you find your way if you ask them. If this has not been your experience, maybe you need to change your approach. Here too, ask someone who finds that most people help him, and see what you can learn.

You might needs words of encouragement. Find someone who can encourage you.

You might need to find a book to read on a topic you would like to know more about. Ask someone in person, call on the telephone, send a letter, or use other means of communication to find what you are looking for.

Be patient when you need to find the appropriate person to

help you. If what you need exists or is known, there will always be someone who will be able to help.

At the same time, be happy to be a resource for others. Every piece of knowledge and information that you have can be valuable to someone else. You might assume that you would not have what to offer others. But just by knowing what you already know, you certainly can help someone. Sharing what you know with others can be yet another source for creating a happy life for yourself.

A very kind middle-aged woman once told me, "I used to be hesitant about asking others for the information that I needed. I could easily consult close friends and relatives. But if I did not know someone well, I did not like to bother them."

"How do you feel about sharing what you know with those who ask you questions?" I asked her.

"I'm grateful for the opportunity to help another person. If I know what they need to know, it's my pleasure to share it."

"So should not you judge others favorably?" I asked. "Why not assume that others are as kind as you are?"

"I never thought of it that way," she replied. "If someone felt about helping me the way I feel about helping them, I would feel fine about asking them."

About a month later, I received a grateful call, "I've asked a number of people questions that previously I would have felt uncomfortable asking. And I also find greater satisfaction in being able to answer others. I see now how being a resource for others gives me a feeling that I have a right to assume that others will be willing to be a resource for me."

87.
MELTING BLOCKS

I used to have more blocks than I do now. Most likely you do also. The blocks that I used to have and do not any longer have melted. So have yours. Melt more blocks to live a more joyous life.

What are your main blocks? These are your limiting beliefs about yourself and your possibilities. These are when you claim, "I cannot," when you really can. These are the abilities that you have manifested at least once and you hesitate to realize that you can do them again. These are the patterns and strengths of others that you have observed, and while you could really model them yourself, you feel that you cannot. These are the positive states that you can really access at will but you believe you cannot.

Let your blocks melt. They are an illusion. If you think there is a wall but it is an illusion, the very act of knowing that it is an illusion melts the block. When you thought that the wall was real, you were stuck. Realizing that it is an illusion lets you go beyond it. My blocks were illusions and so are yours. Melt them.

The more reasons you give for your blocks, the stronger they become. Any block you have is because you have given them a sense of reality and now you can make them disappear.

Think of a specific block you once had and now do not. What can you now do that at one time you could not? It might be public speaking, asking others for favors, asking others to donate money to a worthy cause, learning to perform in some way, speaking another language, confronting someone, overcoming a bad habit, gaining more self-discipline, motivating yourself. The same way you already overcame the blocks that you have already overcome, your brain can also overcome new blocks.

Visualize your blocks melting as ice melts in the sun. See yourself speaking and acting in ways you thought you could not. Feel the joy of knowing that from now on blocks are what you build with. They no longer serve as a wall to box you in. They become a ladder to climb. You become taller and your reach becomes higher.

I have often been told, "It's hard to get rid of blocks and it takes a long time." This, too, is an illusion. When you accept the belief that mental blocks can easily be melted in a short time, your belief breaks them as fast as you accept this belief. Visualize yourself breaking the blocks and act as if they do not exist.

The biggest block is not believing in yourself. Find someone who believes in you. Find someone who believes that every human being can melt every block. And as you see your own blocks melting away, you will become a powerful resource for helping others melt their blocks.

Pray for our Creator to remove your blocks. When you feel blocked, you might feel powerless. This is exactly the time you need to connect with the source of all power. By connecting with the All-powerful, what used to be considered a block will now be yet another opportunity to intensify your spiritual awareness.

Feel joy with every block you overcome. This will create a domino effect and block after block will fall, paving the way for many accomplishments and greater happiness.

88.
ON BEING REAL

Cherish your emotions. Do not be afraid of them. Your emotions are an expression of your true feelings about things. It might not always be appropriate to express them to others, but you yourself will benefit greatly by knowing your true feelings.

People who are in touch with their true feelings live a richer life. They live with more integrity. They have a better understanding of themselves and others. They are the best public speakers and teachers. You can trust such a person more than those who consistently hide their emotions.

When you are afraid, or sad, or upset, or angry, or nervous, be real to yourself. Saying to yourself, "I am afraid right now," or "I am angry," is the first step in overcoming your fear and letting your anger go. Knowing that you are sad or nervous saves you from exerting the energy that you would expend if you were to try to hide your feelings.

Being real with your feelings does not mean that you allow your anger to control you, or your fears to stop you, or your nervousness to rule you, or your sadness to overwhelm you. Rather you acknowledge your distressful feelings, experience them fully, and let them go. This ultimately opens you up to more vitality and energy. You will experience a wider range of emotions. There will be an awareness of pain, but also more joy, greater courage, and self-mastery.

Some people who value happiness tell themselves, "I should never be unhappy," or, "I feel embarrassed that I am not more in control of how I feel." Therefore they think they feel the way they "should" rather than the way they actually do. Our goal is greater mastery of joy, serenity, confidence, courage, empowerment, and being centered and balanced. By being true to yourself, you know when you do experience these emotions and when you do not.

I am forever grateful to my mother who gave me positive feedback for expressing my emotions when I was a little boy. She read me a story with a sad part and I cried. "I'm so glad you have feelings," my mother said to me. This has helped me to be empathic with people who apologize for crying. "There is no need to apologize," I reply. "Your crying is an expression of your ability to experience your feelings."

There is a time for rejoicing and a time to cry or mourn. A basic Torah concept is that each emotion has its time and place. Even if you personally are in the best of states, when talking to someone who is suffering either physically or emotionally, the ideal is to experience this person's suffering with him. Opening your emotional energy and being aware of your actual feelings gives you a greater ability to experience the emotions of others with them.

89.
LIVING HAPPILY EVER AFTER

Everyone has heard of the famous story of the hen that could lay golden eggs. A farmer once bought a hen that looked ordinary, but was really very special. Each day the lucky owner of this hen would find a golden egg instead of merely a plain white one with liquid inside. He was thrilled. His mind was filled with daydreams about all the many things he would do when he had enough golden eggs to create a major fortune.

But then the farmer became impatient. "Why should I wait a long time until the golden eggs add up?" he asked himself. "Let me slaughter the hen today and then I can use all that gold right away."

After slaughtering the special hen, the farmer was shocked. To his great disappointment, there was nothing inside the hen. His impatience had ruined everything.

This story is usually told as a sad one. It wisely warns us not to allow impatience to rob us of what we already have. But it seems to me that there is a lot more to this story. This is a tale that can be told with a happy ending (and I happen to like happy endings, since the feelings engendered are uplifting).

Our farmer felt bad at first. All his great plans had just disappeared into thin air. Then he thought to himself, "If I had not had the good fortune to acquire this hen, I would not feel bad that I no longer own a hen that presented me with golden eggs. So now that I had some good fortune, it does not make sense that I should needlessly make myself feel miserable about what I do not have."

From then on our farmer made a new decision. He was going to be joyously appreciative of whatever he did have. This was a quality that would never be taken away from him. So while he did not get any more golden eggs, he acquired something that was even more precious. He was now the owner of an attitude that would enable him to live happily ever after.

By not focusing on what he was missing, the wise farmer would save himself from much unnecessary distress. By focusing on what he did have, the joyous farmer would always find things to be happy about. This is an attitude that you too can cultivate.

The practice of blessing the Giver of all that you have for what He has given you will increase your skill of appreciating what you have. There are formal blessings. Say them with sincere gratitude and they will effectively enrich your life. And consistently express your gratitude to our Father, our King, Creator and Sustainer of the universe, in your own words for all that you appreciate. When you do this often enough, you too will live happily ever after.

90

UNATTACH ATTACHMENTS

"Someone stole my jewelry and what was most painful was the loss of my great-grandmother's wedding ring."

"Friends keep moving away and this makes me intensely unhappy."

"My computer crashed and I am totally discombobulated."

Attachment makes you emotionally dependent. Become free. Give up your attachments. Allow your happiness in life to be dependent on your own mind and not on anything external.

Attachments are normal. We all become attached to people, possessions, our environment and usual circumstances. A master of happiness will appreciate what he or she has while one has them, and the moment any specific thing is gone or lost the focus will be on other things to appreciate and be grateful for. At times, this could be gratitude for the memories that remain. Material and physical objects are temporary, memories are forever.

A master at non-attachment has nothing to worry about. Worry comes from dependence on things remaining the way you wish them to be.

Some people are concerned, "But if I am not attached to something, I will not enjoy it." Just the opposite. You will enjoy it more while you have it. It is like passing by a beautiful garden or sunset. You enjoy the moment. You do not own it and are not attached to it. Therefore your enjoyment of it is total and complete.

A spiritual consciousness is that as long as it is the will of your benevolent omniscient and omnipotent Father in Heaven that you should have something, you will have it. When your having it has served your ultimate mission in life, you no longer need this. You need other things. And you will always have exactly what you need to fulfill your purpose in this world.

Someone suggested that I give up all feelings of attachment for an entire week. I argued, at first, that this just isn't me. I am very attached to many of the things I own. I would hate to lose the things I consider most precious.

"That's exactly why you need this exercise," he said to me. "You are trapped by what you think is yours. Mentally let go. You're not going to actually lose anything by trying this mental exercise. You can use everything you own. But view them as a tourist or guest would. A tourist enjoys seeing the sights that do not belong to him. A guest in someone's home benefits from the house in which he stays. But he knows it does not belong to him."

This exercise was powerful. When I looked at my watch I appreciated having it more than ever before. I was more grateful for my clothing, for my palm electronic organizer, for my books and my eyeglasses, for my family and my friends. I had taken much of what I had for granted. Viewing them in an unattached way deepened my appreciation for the many things that I was able to utilize and benefit from. I was free from the fear of losing what I had. And this opened me up to a deeper sense of appreciation than I ever had before. I recommend this exercise for everyone. And like I was told, "If you feel you cannot do this, then you must."

91

BOUNCE BACK

No matter how masterful you become at accessing joy, it is almost inevitable that at some time you will fall. We all hit rough spots. We all make mistakes. We all react in ways that we regret. We all find certain situations difficult, even overwhelming. If this ever happens to you, bounce back.

Realize that you have the ability to bounce back quickly. Each moment you make a choice. At any given moment you can empower yourself. How? Think empowering thoughts. Act as if you were energized and empowered. Remember times you felt inner strength and allow yourself to feel those feelings now. See yourself as you were when you felt energized and empowered.

Remember instances when you bounced back. Let this encourage you with the knowledge that you are resilient. Let this give you a sense of total conviction that you already have what it takes to bounce back.

Believe in your Creator's ability to give you renewed strength and energy this very moment. Regardless of how discouraged you have felt, this very moment He can rejuvenate your entire system. Open yourself up to His love for you. Increase your level of trust in His infinite power and compassion. Feel the amazing feelings of knowing that He can save you in the fleeting time it takes to blink an eye.

Nothing was especially wrong with my life. But my biggest problem was that when I had a down, I stayed down. I felt too weak to fight gravity. When I felt like this, I thought that I would always be this way and this made my feelings of despair even stronger.

The turning point for me was when I met an elderly gentleman who was a highly successful businessman. One look at him told you that here was a truly happy person.

"Has life gone easily for you?" I asked him.

"When I look objectively at my life, I have to admit that I had plenty of downs of all kinds. Emotionally, spiritually, and financially I have been down countless times. But I never stayed down. As soon as I was down, I gathered all of my inner strength and got up again. My downs were wake-up calls to strengthen myself."

I did not have to wait very long after this discussion to experience another down. What would have formerly taken a few days to overcome, now took me just a few minutes to conquer. It was amazing. I am now totally aware of how fast I can revitalize myself. I know wholeheartedly that I can do it.

92.
LIST YOUR OWN IDEAS

Y ou are unique. Ideas that works for you and help you increase your happiness and decrease unhappiness might not work for others. And what works for others might not work for you.

Make a list of ideas and techniques that you have found especially helpful. Keep adding to your list.

1. _____

_____

2. _____

_____

3. _____

_____

4. _____

_____

5. _____

_____

6. _____

_____

7. _____

_____

8. _____

_____

9. _____

_____

10. _____

_____

11. _____

_____

12. _____

_____

13. _____

_____

14. _____

_____

15. _____

_____

93.
LIST YOUR JOYOUS MEMORIES

Write a list of your most joyous memories. Whenever you experience joy in the future, add it to your list. These memories are your lifelong resources for joy every time you vividly relive them.

1. _____

2. _____

3. _____

4. _____

5. _____

6. _____

7. _____

8. _____

9. _____

10. _____

11. _____

12. _____

13. _____

14. _____

15. _____

16. _____

17. _____

18. _____

19. _____

20. _____

21. _____

22. _____

23. _____

24. _____

25. _____

26. _____

27. _____

28. _____

29. _____

30. _____

31. _____

32. _____

33. _____

34. _____

35. _____

36. _____

37. _____

38. _____

39. _____

40. _____

41. _____

42. _____

43. _____

44. _____

45. _____

46. _____

47. _____

48. _____

49. _____

50. _____

51. _____

52. _____

53. _____

54. _____

55. _____

56. _____

57. _____

58. _____

59. _____

60. _____

61. _____

62. _____

63. _____

64. _____

65. _____

66. _____

67. _____

68. _____

69. _____

70. _____

71. _____

72. _____

73. _____

74. _____

75. _____